# The Cast Courts

Edited by Angus Patterson
and Marjorie Trusted

V&A Publishing

First published by V&A Publishing, 2018
Victoria and Albert Museum
South Kensington
London SW7 2RL
vam.ac.uk/info/publishing

Distributed in North America by Abrams,
an imprint of ABRAMS

ISBN 9781 85177 9796

10 9 8 7 6 5 4 3 2 1
2022 2021 2020 2019 2018

A catalogue record for this book is available
from the British Library.

Design: planningunit.co.uk
Copy-editor: Denny Hemming
Indexer: Nic Nicholas

New photography by Peter Kelleher

Printed in the UK

Front cover illustration:

Cast of Michelangelo's *David*

Plaster
V&A: Repro.1857–161

Back cover illustration:

Isabel Agnes Cowper (1826–1911)

Construction of the cast of Trajan's Column

Commissioned by Department of Science and Art
of the Committee of Council on Education, 1873

Albumen print
28.2 × 21.8 cm
V&A: 73676

**V&A Publishing**

Supporting the world's leading
museum of art and design,
the Victoria and Albert
Museum, London

# Director's Foreword

John Charles Robinson (1824–1913), the V&A's first curator, travelled extensively across Europe. In 1865, whilst visiting the Spanish pilgrimage site of Santiago de Compostela, he was overawed by the sight of the cathedral's monumental Romanesque portal. Comparing the work to Michelangelo's ceiling in the Sistine Chapel, he insisted on a replica for the South Kensington Museum (as the V&A was then known) – fed by a desire to ensure that many more could view the work despite its remote location.

This great cast is just one of many examples amassed by the authorities at the South Kensington Museum for the dramatic Cast Courts. A source of wonder and an object of study since they first opened in 1873, these spectacular double-height galleries enable visitors to travel thousands of miles, and experience centuries of art history.

For many, including myself, they are still the most memorable galleries in the Museum. Where else could you view the soaring tower of Trajan's Column, situated in Rome, alongside the pugnacious presence of Michelangelo's *David*, which resides in Florence. Nowhere other than in the V&A, in the form of our collection of nineteenth-century casts. Visitors can marvel at the theatrical Gates of Paradise copied from the Baptistery of Florence Cathedral, alongside medieval Scandinavian sculpture from wood stave churches of the eleventh and twelfth centuries. The wealth of digital reproductions now being created has expanded the possibilities of replication, and made us reconsider the potential and benefits of imitation.

We were delighted that the renovation of these imposing and extraordinary spaces came to fruition in 2018, after nearly a decade of curatorial planning, conservation and masterly building work. These galleries have now been returned to their original brilliance, revealing unseen historic features, whilst creating a new interpretation space to place the collection in its broader context.

This compelling book – produced by the curators Angus Patterson and Marjorie Trusted, and their colleagues – conveys something of the casts' history and their relevance today. Through this highly informative and helpful guide, we can better understand the histories, the stories and the ambitions that have – over the course of more than 150 years – shaped the Cast Courts that we see today.

▲

The Weston Cast Court
(room 46B), V&A

▶

The Ruddock Family
Cast Court (room 46A),
V&A

► 

Detail of the punishments
of hell from the Pórtico de la
Gloria, The Ruddock Family
Cast Court (room 46A), V&A

Plaster cast
V&A: Repro.1866–50

Central tympanum
of the Pórtico de la Gloria,
The Ruddock Family Cast
Court (room 46A), V&A

Plaster cast
V&A: Repro.1866–50

# Introduction

'Come', said my friend Professor Omnium, one clear morning, 'let us take an excursion around the world! Go round the world with me here in London.'[1]

When the American writer Moncure Daniel Conway wrote *Travels in South Kensington with Notes on Decorative Art and Architecture in England* in 1882, the Cast Courts of the South Kensington Museum, later to become the Victoria and Albert Museum (V&A), were not yet ten years old. Then known as the Architectural Courts, they exhibited a staggering breadth and wealth of material.

This collection was not merely national; it was international in scope. There was an encyclopaedic sense of completeness engendered by the collection, made possible by the vast and expanding range of copies that complemented original works of art.

◄ (1)

The Ruddock Family
Cast Court (room 46A),
V&A

Today the Cast Courts prompt admiring and
awestruck responses similar to that of Professor
Omnium when visitors walk into them for the first time
(1). The view of the towering bulk of Trajan's Column in
proximity to monumental Italian cathedral doorways
and great Renaissance sculptures is unlike any other
museum gallery. At first sight, this spectacular display
can be mystifying and even confusing.

# Why does the Museum have copies, and why is so much space devoted to their display?

Copies have always been fundamental to the
Museum. These facsimiles sat comfortably alongside
original works because this Victorian encyclopaedia
of international ornament was specifically amassed
to inspire and educate. They were produced for their
forms and decoration, rather than to show their
physical structures. Indeed, they often suggest
materials other than those from which they were
made: painted plaster can deceptively imitate wood,
marble or bronze.

Plaster casting had been practised for centuries,
and the Museum displayed innumerable examples,
alongside the revolutionary nineteenth-century
inventions of photography and electrotyping.
The Museum also displayed brass rubbings, paper
mosaics, watercolours and printed copies of paintings
and architecture as well as architectural models.
The Museum's mission was twofold: to act as a school
of art education for practitioners and to enlighten the
public. First, it aimed to provide the resources to enable
contemporary artists and craftsmen to supply good
designs to Britain's workshops and so improve the
quality of Britain's manufactured products; second,
it aspired to nurture public taste so that consumers
would become more discerning.

Of all the Museum's galleries, the Cast Courts
remain the strongest embodiment of this founding
mission. The Museum's first director, Henry Cole

(1808–1882), prepared the way by instigating an international treaty with the princes of Europe to share works for copying in 1867. Many of the copies in the collection today are the fruits of that agreement.

The Museum's collections of copies also reflect Britain's imperial power in the late nineteenth century. Electrotypes and photographs of African and South-East Asian material were acquired in the 1870s and 1880s. Copies of Indian architectural sculptures were produced in plaster under the supervision of Henry Cole's son, Henry Hardy Cole, in the 1860s and 1870s (2). For the casting of the doorway of the Sanchi Tope, a Buddhist shrine in India, he recorded that 28 tonnes of materials and equipment were transported from Calcutta to Sanchi in 60 carts. The Indian plaster casts were transferred to the Imperial Institute (now Imperial College) in South Kensington at the end of the nineteenth century, but were subsequently destroyed. Today the casts at the V&A are predominantly of European medieval and Renaissance sculptures.

The V&A houses one of the very few cast collections still to be shown in the context built for it. It was not the first such collection – it was preceded by numerous other magnificent groupings of casts in Britain, France, Germany, the Netherlands and elsewhere – but it is one of the few to survive anywhere in the world today. And the V&A's collection, housed in splendid and awe-inspiring spaces, has an undeniably powerful and distinctive character of its own.

The Cast Courts represent a step back in time for visitors today, but in the Victorian era they offered a nineteenth-century vision of both the past and the future. By bringing together of works of art from around the world under one roof, the Museum – and others that followed its lead – created a virtual reality that suggested a new world, more connected and cohesive. Bringing together images and ideas in this way was analogous then to the impact of the internet today. But the scale and physicality of the Cast Courts are most powerful when seen in person: they can still provoke a profound sense of wonder, as strong now as in 1873, when a contributor to *The Builder* magazine marvelled at 'impressions that can scarcely be effaced', and compared seeing the Courts for the first time with 'a first glimpse of Mont Blanc.' [2]

▶ (2)

Isabel Agnes Cowper (1826–1911)

South Kensington Museum, Eastern Cast Court, Victoria and Albert Museum

Commissioned by Department of Science and Art of the Committee of Council on Education

c.1872

Albumen print
27 × 25 cm
V&A: 72507

# The
# Cast Courts

The Cast Courts consist of three spaces: the Weston Cast Court (room 46B), peopled with Italian casts; the Ruddock Family Cast Court (room 46A), which is the Cast Court housing Trajan's Column, as well as numerous medieval casts from Britain, Spain, Germany, France and Scandinavia; and the Chitra Nirmal Sethia Gallery, the arcaded gallery between them (room 46), now housing a display explaining the history of museum reproductions up to the present day.

The existence of these magnificent rooms is one of the reasons the V&A's cast collection survives, while other collections of reproductions in museums elsewhere have been dispersed, or even destroyed.

These galleries have always housed the casts, their scale and decoration reflecting this function. They were designed by Major-General Henry Scott, and inaugurated in 1873. Glass roofs arch over the two main spaces, while the walls of both these galleries are painted in two shades of distemper paint: a warm maroon colour and a mossy green, their original colours. The Weston Cast Court is predominantly green, with maroon borders ( 3 ), while the colours are reversed in the Ruddock Family Cast Court, where the maroon walls are complemented by green borders. Running round the top of the walls of the Ruddock Family Cast Court are gilded cartouches, inscribed with the names of major art centres of the world. Originally cartouches adorned both these galleries, but those in the Weston Cast Court were unfortunately obliterated and lost in the early twentieth century, when a more austere decorative taste prevailed.

▲ (3)

The Weston Cast Court
(room 46B), V&A

The red, black and cream ceramic floor tiles were made by the Crystal Porcelain Pottery Company of Stoke-on-Trent, as recorded in a small contemporary floor panel in the Weston Cast Court (**4**). The mosaic floor of the central gallery was installed by female convicts at Woking Prison, sometimes facetiously dubbed the 'opus criminale'. Both the height and the width of the Courts were dictated by the two largest casts in the collection, which had previously of necessity been accommodated in separate pieces in the Museum. These imposing casts are the two halves of the ancient Roman Trajan's Column (whose total height was 35 metres), each of which reaches up to the roof, and the impressive Pórtico de la Gloria from the Cathedral of Santiago de Compostela (some 41 metres wide), which spans the Courts.

The very architecture of these spaces dictates the ways in which the copies are presented, and the galleries themselves are an indelible part of the visitors' experience. When they were opened, on Thursday 10 July 1873, Henry Cole noted in his diary, 'New Architectural Court opening in Evening. Generally much approved.' This laconic entry underplays the impact of the Courts at the time. Visitors experienced astonishment when they first saw the splendid Cast Courts at South Kensington.

In the days before cheap international travel, and before the era of the well-illustrated art book, copies were fundamental for those who wished to see or learn about works of art elsewhere.

► ( **4** )

Tiled floor in the
Weston Cast Court,
V&A

Originally a vast range of objects was displayed
in the Courts, then known as the Architectural Courts,
together with original sculptures. Brass rubbings,
architectural models and paper mosaics as well as
plaster casts were juxtaposed with a seventeenth-
century alabaster rood loft from 's-Hertogenbosch in
the Netherlands. This array of works of art enabled
visitors to South Kensington to see pieces that were
in reality hundreds of miles apart from each other,
creating a sense of theatre and visual spectacle.

However, after the great era of plaster casts
and copies, made in the late nineteenth century,
some began to express doubts about the value of
reproductions. Applying a mould could damage the
original surface of a sculpture. Moreover, many artists

and students felt it was more important to
derive inspiration from contemporary work,
or the artist's own ideas, rather than through
looking at masterpieces from the past.

During the 1920s and
1930s there were even
threats to the very
survival of the Cast Courts.
It was felt by some that
they could better display
other works of art,
rather than facsimiles.

But when the Second World War broke out in
1939 any thoughts of re-using the spaces were of
necessity abandoned; possibly this national emergency
indirectly saved the Cast Courts and their contents
from destruction. In more recent years the revival of
interest in plaster casts has been palpable. The last
major renovation programme took place in 1981; today,
after the recent restoration of both the spaces and
the collection of casts they house, visitors can
fully appreciate once more the magnificence of the
great Cast Courts.

Only a few years after the Cast Courts were opened
in 1873 a correspondent in *The Times* of 1882 noted
'the most extraordinary jumble of works' at South
Kensington, particularly in comparison with the more
orderly displays of casts at the Kaiser Friedrich Museum
in Berlin. Even today, the profusion of reproductions
on display in the V&A's Cast Courts can be both
exhilarating and daunting. They represent what were
considered in Victorian times to be amongst the most
significant works of European sculpture: monumental
Anglo-Saxon crosses, Spanish Romanesque reliefs,
figures from French Gothic cathedrals, statues by
Italian masters such as Donatello and Michelangelo,

seminally important Flemish and German Renaissance monuments, and the gigantic Trajan's Column from Rome.

These casts were not all acquired at the same time, and came from a variety of sources. They encapsulate the energy and excitement felt by curators wishing to reconstruct a virtual history of European architecture and sculpture within the Museum at South Kensington. The quality and accuracy of these casts meant that they uncannily re-created the exact appearance and scale of the original sculptures. The surface finishes given to the plasters imitate marble, stone, bronze or wood, so that at first glance many are indistinguishable from the originals from which they were cast.

European plaster cast collections have existed since the sixteenth century. Numerous royal collectors, such as Francis I of France, in the 1530s, and Philip IV of Spain, in the 1640s, amassed plaster copies of canonical classical sculptures from Rome. Likewise, aristocrats were proud to acquire and display plaster casts of the most celebrated antique marbles in their libraries and reception rooms during the eighteenth and nineteenth centuries. Meanwhile art academies all over Europe assembled plaster reproductions for students to copy. The Royal Academy of Arts in London, for example, possesses a large and impressive collection of casts dating back to the 1770s. The École des Beaux Arts in Paris owned a range of plaster casts from the 1830s onwards. Individual architects and artists, such as the architect Sir John Soane (1753–1837) in London, and the painter Johann Raphael Mengs (1717–1768) in Dresden, acquired plaster casts for their own study, and in order to teach students. Most of these were reproductions of classical sculptures, but by the mid-nineteenth century plaster casts were being made of post-classical monuments and sculpture.

In 1837 the Government School of Design was established at Somerset House in London, and acquired a collection of 'casts of ornamental art of all periods and countries' for teaching purposes. This collection, which was rich in casts of medieval pieces, was taken over by the Museum soon after it was founded in 1852. In 1857 a large collection of Gothic architectural casts was lent to the Museum by the Royal Architectural Museum, then also in South Kensington. Although these were returned in 1869, from 1916 they became part of the permanent collection of the V&A.

▲ (**5**)

Giovanni Franchi & Son
(*fl*.1857–76)

Cast of the pulpit for
the Baptistery in Pisa,
by Nicola Pisano

1260 (sculpted), *c*.1864 (cast)

Plaster
Height: 462.5 cm
V&A: Repro.1865–52

▲ (**6**)

Cast of a portrait bust of
a woman, by Francesco
Laurana

1472 (sculpted), *c.*1889 (cast)

Plaster
51 × 46 cm
V&A: Repro.1889–94

In addition to these decorative and architectural casts, from the 1850s onwards the Museum also acquired exceptional examples of medieval and Renaissance sculpture, such as Nicola Pisano's thirteenth-century pulpit from Pisa ( **5** ), Jacopo della Quercia's fifteenth-century portal from the Basilica of San Petronio in Bologna, part of the fifteenth-century Rosslyn Chapel in Scotland, and Master Mateo's twelfth-century Pórtico de la Gloria from Santiago de Compostela in Spain (see pp.46–51).

Often the Museum would specially commission such casts to be made by plaster cast makers (*formatori*) based in London, such as Giovanni Franchi (*c*.1812–1874) or Domenico Brucciani (1815–1880). The Museum's first curator, John Charles Robinson, was a particularly active collector of casts on behalf of the Museum, and it was he who commissioned Brucciani, for instance, to make the cast of the Pórtico de la Gloria. Sometimes casts were presented to the Museum, such as Michelangelo's *David*, which had been given by Queen Victoria as early as 1857. On occasion casts were purchased from plaster cast makers in Italy or Germany, such as those acquired from the Milanese masters Pietro Pierotti and Carlo Campi in the 1860s and 1890s.

In 1867 a 'Convention for Promoting Universally Reproductions of Works of Art for the Benefit of Museums of All Countries' was instigated by Henry Cole at the Exposition Universelle (World Fair) in Paris and signed by 15 European princes. It heralded a new era of international cooperation between museums and generated vast numbers of copies that were sold, lent and exchanged around the world. For example, a cast of a bust by the Italian Renaissance sculptor Francesco Laurana (*c*.1430–1502), owned by the Kaiser Friedrich Museum, was copied for South Kensington using the mould in Berlin ( **6** ).

The Convention championed the new replicating technologies of photography and electrotyping, revolutionary combinations of art and science that complemented traditional plaster casting. The Museum set up its first Photographic Studio as early as 1853, when photography was still an extremely recent phenomenon. This blend of science and art enabled accurate reproductions to be made without the need for direct contact with an original work. Three years later the National Art Library in the Museum began collecting and sharing photographs of places, architecture and works of art from far and wide to provide reference images for students and designers. Photographs were relatively cheap to produce, transport and store; they were collected and exchanged in great numbers. Additionally, travellers and explorers gave or sold photographs to the Museum, or lent their own negatives to be printed. Prints of objects on loan to the Museum joined the Photographs Collection.

Electrotyping was a nineteenth-century alchemy, a product of an electrical revolution that enabled the material world to be manipulated and reproduced at a molecular level. It produced multiple copies that were accurate, robust and portable. This new process was developed at the same time as photography, recording external surfaces rather than internal structures. Electrotype copies are in effect three-dimensional photographs.

The process was developed and patented by Elkington & Co. of Birmingham, a company with whom the Museum worked closely for 70 years.

Cast makers Giovanni Franchi & Son also supplied electrotypes, and when Franchi died Elkington bought his business and became the sole English supplier to the Museum.

The recent developments of digital scanning, photogrammetry and 3D printing have prompted museums and cultural heritage organizations to look afresh at the 1867 Convention. In 2017 the Reproduction of Art and Cultural Heritage (ReACH) Project marked the 150th anniversary of the Convention by launching a new agreement for the digital age, linking heritage organizations around the world and encouraging them to record and protect archaeological sites at risk.

# Plaster Casts, Electrotypes and Photographs

# Michelangelo's *David*

◄ ( **7** )

Cast of Michelangelo's
*David*, displayed in
the Weston Cast Court
(room 46B), V&A

The giant plaster cast of Michelangelo's *David* was
a gift offered in consolation. Leopold II, Grand Duke of
Tuscany, sent the cast to Queen Victoria after refusing
to allow the export of a painting by Ghirlandaio, which
the National Gallery had hoped to acquire. The Queen
donated the cast to the South Kensington Museum in
1857, where it was one of the first objects to be installed
in its new buildings ( **7** ).[1]

The Grand Duke's gift travelled to Britain in three
wooden crates, on a 155-tonne ship named the *Cheshire
Witch*. Large, modern exhibition rooms were needed to
display the gigantic figure of *David*, which measures
over 5 metres in height. The Museum's first director,
Henry Cole, saw the assembly of the cast and noted the
occasion in his diary on 21 February 1857: 'Mr Cowper
remained till 4.30 & saw the legs of *David* erected,
not without jeopardy...' ( **8** ). The cast was given
a prominent position in the ground floor gallery,
where it overlooked other Italian sculptures from
its tall wooden pedestal ( **9** ). Four months later,
on 20 June 1857, the Museum was opened to the public.
Students, artists and craftsmen could now admire the
faithful copy of Michelangelo's masterpiece in London
without the need to travel to Italy.

In the 1870s the cast of *David* was moved to the
new Cast Courts, in what was then the Eastern Court
(today the Weston Cast Court), where it was later
displayed in front of the monumental cast of Jacopo
della Quercia's great fifteenth-century portal from the
Basilica of San Petronio, Bologna, to be acquired in
1886. It was subsequently moved to the other end of
the gallery, where it stood in front of the south wall
until 2012, when it was given a more prominent
position, on the gallery's central axis. This is where
it stands today, surrounded by other copies of
Michelangelo's masterpieces.

The story of the cast begins in 1847, when officials in Florence decided to move the original marble figure of *David*, then standing in the Piazza della Signoria in Florence, as it was suffering from weathering in its exposed position outdoors. The Grand Duke commissioned a royal cast maker and bronze founder, Clemente Papi (1803–1875), to make a mould of the original marble, and produce an exact copy of Michelangelo's sculpture. This replica would be used to determine a suitable place to which the original marble might be moved.[2]

To create the replica Papi produced over 1,500 piece-moulds of sections of the figure, cast directly from the marble's surface, which had been sealed with oil, wax or soap to help release the plaster.[3] The piece-moulds were different sizes and shapes, and they were arranged on the sculpture's surface like a jigsaw, with each section being held in place by mother-moulds, also made of plaster. Papi's moulding process is still visible on the surface of the V&A cast as a network of raised seam lines.

# The cast captures the condition of the original marble as it was in 1847, when the mould was taken.

The head and shoulders are pitted in areas where the marble had suffered from erosion and cracks on the original marble can be seen on the surface of the tree stump behind his left leg. Some of this detail was subsequently obscured by the application of three layers of lead-based paint, although it has now been revealed once more after careful cleaning and conservation.

▶ (**8**)

View of the interior of the South Kensington Museum, the boilerhouse, featuring the cast of *David*

1860s

▶ (**9**)

Charles Thurston Thompson (1816–1868)

Interior view of a display space with a galleried wall. There is an engine mounted on wheels in the foreground. In the background can be seen the lower portion of the cast of *David*

Commissioned by Department of Science and Art of the Committee of Council on Education

1856

Albumen print
24.8 × 28.5 cm
V&A: E.1074–1989

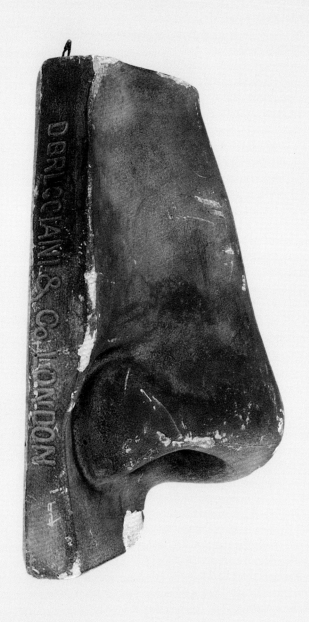

Papi reinforced the cast with metal rods to ensure the figure could be supported by its legs and the tree stump. The cast weighs less than a quarter of the original marble, and X-rays have revealed that the metal rods supporting the legs were arranged similarly to human leg bones. To increase the structural stability, the cavities inside the legs were filled with plaster, while the torso and head were left hollow. Papi also designed the cast so that it could be dismantled and reassembled; this explains the visible joints.

Papi's methods enabled multiple copies of the sculpture of *David* to be produced, both as a whole figure and in parts. He made three full-scale copies of the work from his original mould. After completing his second plaster cast for Queen Victoria in 1856, he cast a third copy in bronze ten years later, which was – and still is – displayed at the Piazzale Michelangelo in Florence. Papi also created a bronze head, now lost, from the original mould, as well as a plaster head, which is on display at the Accademia di Belle Arti (Academy of Fine Arts) in Florence .[4]

Papi's original moulds do not survive, although later moulds of the sculpture were made by other cast makers. The Anglo-Italian, London-based cast maker, Domenico Brucciani, made a mould from Papi's cast in 1857 together with additional copies of the head, nose, eyes, ears and lips, some of which are in the V&A collection (**10**).[5] The V&A collection also includes Brucciani's fig leaf, a replacement for Papi's original fig leaf, which had been lost. Fig leaves were often used to conceal the nudity of sculptures in the nineteenth century. Early photographs of the original marble and Papi's bronze copy at Piazzale Michelangelo show that both those sculptures were likewise adorned with fig leaves.

Today casts of *David* continue to inspire creativity. The development of 3D scanning allows potential for the figure to be produced by 3D printing from digital renderings. In 2017 film-goers around the world would have seen a full-size model constructed from digital scans of the V&A's cast in Ridley Scott's film *Alien: Covenant*.

◄ (**10**)

D. Brucciani & Co., London
(*fl*.1851–1915)

Cast of the nose of
Michelangelo's *David*

1891 (cast)

Plaster
V&A: Repro.1891–43
Photograph: George Eksts
© Victoria and Albert Museum,
London

1. Bucca fatta scavare da Sisto V. con ricinto
di muro, e Scala, che discende al piano della Colonna.

*Colonna Trajana*

2. Chiesa del Nome di Maria.
3. Palazzo Bonelli.

Piranesi fecit

# Trajan's Column

◄ (11)

Giovanni Battista Piranesi
(1720–1778)

Trajan's Column, Rome

*c.*1760–78

Etching
54.8 × 41 cm
V&A: CAI.933

Some copies have become almost as famous as the original works from which they were cast. The towering presence of Trajan's Column, shown in two halves in a gallery whose height was determined by its display, dominates the Ruddock Family Cast Court. It is one of the most impressive casts in the V&A's collection and represents a tremendous feat of moulding electrotyping, casting and engineering. The cast reproduces one of the earliest dated examples of sculpture in the cast collection, an ancient Roman monument, and has been on display in its present form since the opening of the Cast Courts (then known as the Architectural Courts) in 1873.

The original Trajan's Column was erected in marble to commemorate the two successful campaigns of the Emperor Trajan against the Dacians along the Danube frontier in AD 101–2 and 105–6. It may have been designed and constructed under the supervision of the architect Apollodorus of Damascus, and has since stood at the focal point of the Forum in Rome. The Doric column depicts the history of Trajan's campaigns in a spiralling low relief frieze, which winds round the column for a total length, if it could be unfurled, of over 200 metres. It depicts 155 scenes and over 2,500 individual figures ( **11** ).

Plaster moulds were taken from the original column in 1861–2 for Emperor Napoleon III. They were sent to the workshop of the pioneering Parisian founder, Leopold Oudry (*fl.*1854–*c.*1882), so that he could make copper electrotypes in them. The technique of electrotyping, the deposition of copper at a molecular level into moulds using electricity, was not yet 25 years old and Trajan's Column was the largest commission by this process to that date. The electrotypes were once displayed at the Musée du Louvre, but now survive in parts at the Château of St Germain en Laye, outside Paris.

► (**12**)

Isabel Agnes Cowper
(1826–1911)

Construction of the cast
of Trajan's Column, with
choir screen from the
Cathedral of St John
's-Hertogenbosch, the
Netherlands, in the
background

Commissioned by
Department of Science and
Art of the Committee of
Council on Education

1873

Albumen print
28.2 × 21.8 cm
V&A: 73676

► (**13**)

View of the interior of the
Western Architectural
Court in the Victoria and
Albert Museum, taken
from the South Gallery

1873

Watercolour
40.3 × 30.4 cm
V&A: D.564–1905

The electrotypes were used as patterns from which the V&A's plaster casts were made in 1864 at a cost of £2,498 11s. 2d. The Museum's Trajan's Column is therefore a copy of a copy. Old and new methods of copying complemented each other. Casting from electrotypes was not uncommon, nor was electrotyping from plaster casts, and both were photographed.

Commissioning casts of the base of the plinth seems to have been an afterthought and was further delayed as the electrotypes of the base had become buckled in Paris and had to be straightened before the casts could be made.[1] These casts were eventually completed by M. Maitre in 1872 at a cost of 5,000 francs.

When the casts were first acquired by the South Kensington Museum (as the V&A was then known) in the 1860s, they could not be accommodated on high columns as they are now and were instead displayed in sections mounted on smaller structures. In 1873 the Cast Courts were completed and were built to a height of 25 metres, specifically to accommodate the column in two parts.[2] *The Art Journal* commented that, 'The march of the warriors of Rome will come to a sudden conclusion at the glass-ceiling, but will recommence on the floor of the court.'[3]

Two brick cores were built to support the plaster reliefs, necessary at such a height, at a cost estimated by George Smith and Co. of £233.[4] Each section of relief is approximately 1.2 m high, 0.6 m wide and about 2.5 cm thick, and is individually numbered. A photograph by one of the Museum's earliest photographers, Isabel Agnes Cowper (1826–1911), shows the column being assembled piece by piece, like a giant jigsaw puzzle, around the brick core (12).

The construction of the column was finally completed in 1874, a year after the Cast Courts opened. An anonymous late nineteenth-century watercolour of the Western Court depicts the original decorative scheme, and clearly shows the scale of the cast in comparison with the other copies around it (13). The watercolour also depicts the upper half of the column topped by the bronze figure of St Peter, which surmounts the marble column in Rome, but this was not reproduced for the Museum's cast.

The display of Trajan's Column at the Museum has enabled successive students, scholars and visitors to study and admire this great relic of the classical world in Britain. During the nineteenth century it provided a practical alternative to visiting the original monument in Rome. Moreover, while the original has suffered greatly from pollution, the Museum's cast retains much of this now-lost detail. Its display in two halves enables a closer study of the entire frieze.

The cast's reproduction of the classical text used for the inscription on the base was of particular interest (**14**). By 1900 posters and shop signs were changing the urban landscape, giving the graphic arts higher visibility. Increasing literacy boosted the circulation of newspapers and journals. Copies of historic lettering encouraged designers to develop new typefaces integrating lettering and ornament for the expanding printing industry. The letterforms used on Trajan's Column were widely copied, re-used and celebrated, and the convenience of the cast's location – in South Kensington – aided this popularity.[5]

D. Brucciani & Co., the London-based plaster casting firm, sold copies of the lettering for £7 a panel, and many schools of art used these as teaching aids.[6]

The lettering continues to inspire modern typefaces, and the cast continues to be much studied by students of archaeology, art history and calligraphy.

▲ (**14**)

C. Smith & Sons (*fl.*1909-52)

Plaster cast reproducing the Trajan typeface; the original in stone was made by Eric Gill in the early twentieth century

1919

Plaster cast
44 × 29 × 2.5 cm
V&A: Repro.1919–3

PORTAL CALLED "LA GLORIA" WEST END OF CATHEDRAL OF SANTIAGO DE COMPOSTELLA.

THE WORK OF MAESTRO MATIAS AD 1188.

Inscription under the lintel, or soffit of the centre arch

"Ano ab incarnatione Dni M CLXXXVIII era ICCXXVII die KL
aprilis superliminaria principalium portalium"
ecclesie beati Jacobi sunt collocata p. Magistrum Matheum
qui a fundamentis ipsorum portalium gessit magisterium"

POR DIOS    SEÑOR

Y    SANTIAGO.

J.C. Robinson

Santiago Oct. 21
186

# The Pórtico de la Gloria

◄ ( **15** )

John Charles Robinson
(1824–1913)

Sketch drawing of the
Pórtico de la Gloria

1865

Graphite on laid paper
V&A: Reports MA/3/16

As part of his remit to travel extensively across Europe, identifying works either for acquisition or reproduction for the South Kensington Museum, John Charles Robinson, its first curator, made several trips to Spain. In 1865 he travelled to Santiago de Compostela, the capital of the north-western region of Galicia. There he visited the cathedral, dedicated to St James (Santiago) the Apostle, one of the most important European centres of pilgrimage since medieval times.[1] He was overawed by the sight of the Pórtico de la Gloria, the cathedral's monumental Romanesque portal, profusely decorated with figures and reliefs carved skilfully out of granite, most of whose rich colouring still survived.

The Pórtico had been constructed at the end of the twelfth century under the patronage of Ferdinand II of León, commissioned from the sculptor and architect Maestro Mateo.[2] The structure is arranged as three arches with a central, monumental tympanum supported by a decorated mullion and serves as the main entrance to the cathedral ( **15** ). The decorative scenes depict St John's Vision of the Apocalypse, the end of the known world, with a triumphant Christ at its centre establishing the eternal Kingdom of God or the celestial Jerusalem.[3] The sculptures capture this moment: the 24 Elders of the Apocalypse on the main arch appear to converse animatedly, while tuning their musical instruments in readiness for playing a new song for a new era, led by Christ enthroned, who shows the wounds of the Passion.

Robinson compared this work favourably with Michelangelo's ceiling in the Sistine Chapel at the Vatican, and Lorenzo Ghiberti's Gates of Paradise in Florence, championing it as one of the most outstanding examples of Romanesque art in Europe. He urged Henry Cole, the director of the Museum, to commission a replica, recommending that a watercolourist should capture the elaborate paint scheme in colour. He argued that the remoteness of its location would make it inaccessible to many students and art lovers, making it imperative to have a copy for display in the Museum. Robinson stated, 'I consider it incomparably the most important monument of sculpture and ornamental detail of its epoch, the 12th century, I have ever seen or heard of.'[4]

Cole commissioned the cast from Domenico Brucciani, one of many Italian cast makers working in London whose new gallery of casts, his Galleria delle Belle Arti, opened in Covent Garden in 1864. In November 1865 Brucciani travelled to Santiago to study the work and make plans and elevations for the moulding and casting. He had to explain his methods repeatedly to the authorities in Spain, assuring them that the Pórtico would not be damaged. Eventually the Archbishop and Dean of the Cathedral, and the Real Academia de Bellas Artes (Royal Academy of Fine Arts), of San Fernando in Madrid granted him permission to undertake the work.

On 2 July 1866 Brucciani set off from London by boat with all the necessary materials and a team of workmen. Their trip to the north-west coast of Spain was more hazardous than anticipated. They endured rough seas and stormy weather, a collision with a barge, a fire on the ship and a forced stay in the quarantine station on San Simón, an island in the bay of Vigo, to prevent any possible spread of the cholera pandemic affecting the East End of London at the time.

We know little of Brucciani's methods for moulding such a monumental work, although documentary evidence suggests he used foils, clay, plaster and fabric.[5] 'Mr Brucciani proposes to cover the highly sculptured details of the work with their foils and other substances impermeable by moisture, so that the clay and plaster employed in making the moulds will not be in contact with the sculpture's surfaces,' reported Robinson.[6]

As the moulds had to be taken directly from the surface of the original portal, local officials and the inhabitants of Santiago were anxious about possible damage, particularly to the surviving polychrome. Brucciani was therefore directed by the Academia in Madrid to work under the supervision of the Professor

► (16)

Isabel Agnes Cowper
(1826–1911)

Cast of the Pórtico de la Gloria

1873

Albumen print
58.8 × 37 cm
V&A: 73128

of Drawing at the University of Santiago, and also painter, Juan José Cancela del Río.[7]

Evidence found during recent conservation indicates that Brucciani covered areas of the original with linseed oil and a protective layer of fabric, before moulding the surface in plaster to produce piece-moulds.[8] This is a traditional technique less harmful for the polychrome and the granite on the Pórtico, and far safer than gelatin moulds, an alternative method also widely used at the time to mould large and complex surfaces. Due to the speed of Brucciani's team, the resulting casts necessitated extensive reworking of their surfaces to remove imperfections, transferring a certain lack of definition to some areas of the cast. Therein lies the tension when making moulded replicas. All moulded copies are approximations of the original works, with varying degrees of accuracy. The more a copy is reworked by hand to look like the original, the further it strays from the initial rendering, giving the copy its own quality and character.

Remarkably, Brucciani and his team completed the moulding and casting in just over two months. Before shipping the casts to London Brucciani exhibited his

▲ (**17**)

Cast of the Pórtico de la
Gloria, on display at the
Exposición Internacional
(World Fair), Barcelona, 1929

L'Arxiu Fotografic de Barcelona

work inside the cathedral for the people of Santiago to admire, 'forming a small Gallery of Art ... no less than seven thousand persons passed through the Cathedral inspecting the work which they showed their approbation by their repeated exclamations of gratifications.'[9] When the casts arrived at the Museum they were displayed in sections. It was not until 1873, when the Cast Courts were built, their width determined by this great cast, that the Pórtico could be displayed in all its glory. It has been studied and admired in South Kensington ever since.

The legacy of the Pórtico cast would be experienced beyond London. Further moulds were taken from the cast by the Museum's Casting Service, led by Paul Joseph Ryan, Brucciani's grandson, in the early twentieth century. Partial copies were produced to be displayed at the Museo de Reproducciones (Museum of Artistic Reproductions) in Madrid in 1926, and an entire cast of the Pórtico went on display at the Exposición Internacional (World Fair) in Barcelona in 1929 (**17**). It has continued to be a source of inspiration far away from its place of origin in Galicia.

Cast of an arabesque
roundel from the prayer hall,
Madrasa of Sultan Hasan,
Cairo (AD 1356–63)

1884 (cast)

Plaster
76.2 × 4 cm
V&A: Repro.1884–827

# Islamic Ornament

In the late nineteenth century the South Kensington Museum deliberately sought to acquire casts of Islamic ornament, in order to be as comprehensive as possible in its aim to form 'an historical museum of ornament.'[1] The best of Islamic architecture was exemplified by two sets of buildings: the Islamic palace complex of the Alhambra in Granada (fourteenth century) and the masterpieces of Mamluk Cairo (1250–1517). It was the monuments of the fourteenth and fifteenth centuries that were most greatly admired.

Since its foundation in 1852 the Museum had collected a wide range of material, including plaster casts, from the Alhambra. In 1883 the Museum acquired 50 casts of Alhambra ornament from the Real Academia de la Historia (Royal Academy of History) in Madrid, facilitated by Juan Facundo Riaño (1829–1901), the Spanish academic and adviser to the Museum.[2] These were then displayed in the Cast Courts, under the arches of the Pórtico de la Gloria.[3]

In the case of Egypt, the Museum commissioned experts who were travelling there to take papier mâché 'squeezes' (moulds), which were subsequently turned into casts at the Museum ( 18 ). In 1871 one such mission was undertaken by the clergyman and collector Reverend Greville Chester (1830–1892), who during his career also acquired objects for the British Museum and the Ashmolean Museum.[4] Another expedition was undertaken in 1883 by Stanley Lane-Poole (1854–1931), an Arabist who acted as adviser to the Museum on 'Saracenic' art.[5] In the publication that resulted from Lane-Poole's mission, he describes how he 'took casts of ... ornament, and was fortunately able to bring back paper squeezes, fortified with layers of gypsum, of every distinct ornament on the whole façade. From these squeezes plaster casts have been made, and a set of these are now exhibited in the gallery over the architectural court of the South Kensington Museum'.[6]

One building that seems to have been particularly favoured by European visitors to Cairo was the Wikala (a combined warehouse, retail space and hostel for merchants) erected by Sultan Qa'itbay (r. 1468–96) in 1477. Lane-Poole described this building as 'almost a text-book of Saracenic decoration' (**19**).[7] This 'text-book' aspect would have appealed to the Museum's curators in their quest to acquire examples of ornament that could be used in the training of art students. However, by the same token, these ornamental elements were seen out of their geographical context, divorced from any sense of architectural support, so that students had to focus on the 'abstract consideration of the art itself'.[8] The large number of casts from the Wikala that eventually entered the Museum's collections meant that much of its facade could be recreated in the displays at South Kensington.

Lane-Poole may have been advised on what to cast by the architect James Wild (1814–1892), brother-in-law of the architect and design theorist Owen Jones, as he is thanked in the introduction to Lane-Poole's book. Wild had visited Cairo in the 1840s, and his surviving sketchbooks contain drawings of ornament that relate to casts the Museum acquired 40 years later.[9] He may effectively have written a shopping list for South Kensington.

In 1884 the Museum acquired almost wholesale the collection of Count Gaston de Saint-Maurice (1831–1905), who was equerry to the Khedive (Ottoman governor) of Egypt. Along with other French aristocrats based in Cairo, Saint-Maurice lived in a 'maison arabe', designed and built for him between 1872 and 1879 by the French architect Ambroise Baudry (1838–1906).[10] This housed his collection of Islamic art, while its walls were decorated with plaster casts taken from different Cairene monuments.

Saint-Maurice exhibited his collection at the 1878 Exposition Universelle in Paris, in the section titled 'Egypte des Khalifes',[11] where it was seen and its quality commented on by South Kensington curators. A memorandum preserved in the V&A Archive highlights, 'a very important group ... of casts in fibrous plaster of some of the finest portions of the ceilings,

▶ (**19**)

Pascal-Xavier Coste
(1787–1879)

Study drawing of the
Wikala of Sultan Qa'itbay

Preparatory illustration
for *Architecture Arabe,
ou Monuments du Kaire*
(Paris, 1837 and 1839)

1818–22

Pencil, pen and ink,
wash and watercolour
58 × 44.5 cm
V&A: SD.272:32

▶ (**20**)

Section of a ceiling,
from a house in Cairo

1872–9 (cast)

Plaster and pigment
200 × 200 cm (approx.)
V&A: 1884–1030C

VUE DE LA PORTE ET DÉTAILS DES BOUTIQUES DE L'OGEL DE QAYD-BEY.

niches and heads of doorways of the principal buildings in Cairo.' Some of these were coloured. 'Where the originals are coloured all the decorations are artistically reproduced; and in all cases where portions only are given, these portions are quarters so as to allow for the completion of the whole objects without trouble or mistake' (**20**).[12]

► (**21**)

*Catalogue of Casts for Schools*, 1922 edition, plate 14

These casts were made locally in Cairo, and have a soft pink plaster body incorporating wood and straw to bind and strengthen them, but are nevertheless very fragile.

They have not survived well in the 150 years since they were made. In fact they were re-cast in Plaster of Paris when they arrived at South Kensington, thus creating multiples of the same examples of ornament, copies of copies. The Museum dispersed these multiples to the museums in Dublin and Edinburgh – in accordance with its role as the Central Museum of Ornamental Art – as well as to regional schools of design. The 1922 *Catalogue of Casts for Schools*, produced by D. Brucciani & Co., features among the casts cited as examples of good design an 'Arabian capital', from the Alhambra, as number 233 and an 'Arabesque Panel, [from] Cairo', as number 238 (**21**). Surrounded by their Gothic and Renaissance counterparts, these works were singled out as representing the best of Islamic ornament, to be admired and imitated, and widely disseminated throughout regional museums and design schools.

189    229    222    231    232

238    233    370    314    272    307

394    237    308    346    382    344    345

347    348    371    379

57

# Scandinavian Casts

◂ (22)

Cast of a wooden doorway
from Urnes, Norway

1050–70 (made)
*c*.1907 (cast)

Plaster
Height: 274.5 cm
V&A: Repro.1907–58

Britain had a love affair with medieval Scandinavian sculpture in the late nineteenth and early twentieth centuries, illustrated by the numerous plaster casts from Norway and Sweden now on view in the Cast Courts. Norwegian and Swedish wood stave churches of the eleventh and twelfth centuries were greatly admired by the British, in particular the grotesque intertwined beasts depicted on the churches' portals. They were named 'stave' churches after the wood staves or supports used in their construction. Normally built of pine, they were originally painted red, white and black, although the original colours have no longer survived.

Of the many hundreds of such wood churches once in existence in Scandinavia only a few dozen had survived by the second half of the nineteenth century, and in 1867 some of the portals were exhibited at the Exposition Universelle held in Paris.

Two of the most celebrated of these medieval churches were those of Urnes and Flå, just north of Oslo. The authorities at the South Kensington Museum (later the Victoria and Albert Museum) had plaster copies made from the portal ornaments, and they are today proudly displayed in the Cast Courts (22). The exact meaning of these intricate entwined creatures and foliage is not fully understood.

In addition the Museum acquired at much the same time plaster casts of medieval Swedish fonts, and a tomb from Botkyrka in Sweden, dating from the early twelfth century (23 & 24). These plaster reproductions were evidently of enormous interest to the Victorians, partly because the originals from which they were cast seemed to form a link with the Viking past, although in fact they were made after the Viking era. Scandinavian art across a range of materials had a profound influence on the Arts and Crafts Movement in Britain.

During the early twentieth century, at the height of Art Nouveau, contemporary wood furniture was made in the style of these medieval pieces, notably a chair made for the author of the Sherlock Holmes stories, Sir Arthur Conan Doyle.

◄ (**23**)

Cast of a stone font, now
in the National Museum,
Stockholm

12th century (sculpted)
*c.*1885 (cast)

Plaster
69 × 64 cm
V&A: Repro.1885–201

◄ (**24**)

Cast of a stone font, now
in the National Museum,
Stockholm

12th century (sculpted)
*c.*1885 (cast)

Plaster
91.5 × 77.5 cm
V&A: Repro.1885–202

# The Milton Shield

◄ (25)

Léonard Morel-Ladeuil
(1815–1888) for Elkington & Co.

The original Milton Shield

1866

Steel, inset with silver plaques,
inlaid with gold wire and oxidized
87.6 × 67.3 cm
V&A: 546–1868

'Every face expresses the appropriate mental emotion or passion. There is awe and fear expressed in the face of Adam, and modesty in that of Eve, as they listen to the recital by Raphael of the conflict between the hosts of Heaven and Hell... There is Michael-Angelo-like force of drawing in the terrified faces and forms of the defeated rebels...

## ... How fiercely St Michael wields his flaming sword, as he stands on the prostrate body of the Dragon!' [1]

In his poetic description of the Milton Shield, George Wallis, First Keeper of Fine Art at the South Kensington Museum (now the V&A), was not alone in lauding one of the nineteenth century's great metal masterpieces and expressing its instant appeal to art schools. The original Milton Shield commemorated the 200th anniversary of the publication of John Milton's *Paradise Lost*, his epic biblical narration written at a time of great turmoil after the Civil War. The shield was shown by Elkington & Co. at the Exposition Universelle in Paris of 1867 (25).[2] *The Art Journal* illustrated it and declared, 'There is a general impression that the work here engraved is the best work exhibited during the memorable year of 1867.'[3] *The Times* noted there was 'always a crowd of admirers around it. The work in it is of the finest quality, and the ideas which are expressed in that work are not only full of poetry, but sometimes also reach even to the sublime.'[4]

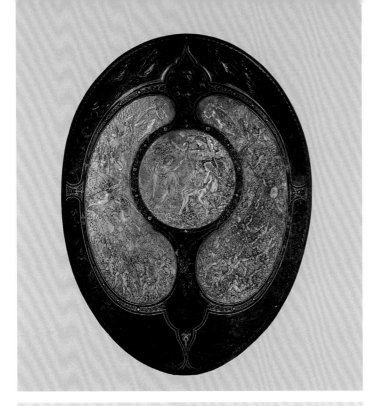

◄ (**26**)

Elkington & Co.,
Birmingham or London

Electrotype of
the Milton Shield

1868

Electroformed copper,
electroplated, electrogilded
and oxidized
V&A: Repro.138–1868

◄ (**27**)

Electrotype of the
Milton Shield, as advertised
in the *Illustrated Catalogue
of Electrotype Reproductions
of Works of Art From Originals
in the South Kensington Museum*,
Science and Art Department
of the Committee of Council
on Education, South
Kensington Museum,
London, 1873

The Museum bought the original shield in 1868 for the huge sum of £2,000 (about £1,500,000 today), and immediately commissioned four electrotype copies of it for use in the art schools, either at South Kensington or for circulation around the country (**26**).[5] An additional copy, dating from 1886 and mounted to a hinged easel, shows how the shield was intended to be seen, close-up at eye level. These electrotypes are perfect impressions of the front surface of the original shield, each electroformed in copper from moulds of the original, and plated, oxidized and gilded to mimic the surface colours of steel, silver and gold. The Museum advertised electrotypes of the shield for sale in 1873, and to do so used another innovative and scientific means of reproduction: photography (**27**). The highest quality copies of 'this noble work of art' were priced in the catalogue at 12 guineas each. Cheaper versions were also sold in plain electroplate and bronzed (copper sulphate) finishes.

The original shield was probably made with replication in mind. Its copies epitomize the methods of large industrial art manufacturers like Elkington, and their appeal to museums modelled on that of South Kensington. Elkington revived labour-intensive, historic techniques by producing expensive and virtuoso artworks for display at international exhibitions. Simultaneously, they expedited those processes through scientific and mechanical means, creating replicas in less expensive materials for a wider market.

The original Milton Shield, the best-known work of the brilliant French repoussé sculptor Léonard Morel-Ladeuil (1815–1888), is a tour de force of intricate steel and silver chasing and gold inlay, skills inspired by the works of Renaissance armourers and goldsmiths. Morel-Ladeuil had been a pupil in Paris of the great historicist and steel chaser Antoine Vechte (1799–1868) before coming to England in 1859 to work for Elkington. Elkington then replicated the shield in copper using electroforming, electroplating and electrogilding techniques. The company had invested heavily in developing, patenting and licensing such techniques to other manufacturers. Hundreds of electrotypes of the Milton Shield, in a variety of finishes, entered international collections. Buyers included major museums in Boston, New York, Paris,

Vienna and Sydney, as well as the White House in Washington, D.C. Private collectors and wealthy industrialists bought copies to furnish their homes.

The popularity of the shield grew. An electrotype of it was shown at the Weltausstellung, Vienna's World Fair, of 1873, and it attracted universal approval once again when an electrotype adorned Elkington's stand at the 1876 Centennial Exhibition in Philadelphia. For post-Civil War America, the shield resonated powerfully with fresh memories of political strife and social upheaval. Although Morel-Ladeuil had created an extraordinarily beautiful new piece for the exhibition *The Pompeian Lady Plaque*,[6] sales of electrotypes of the Milton Shield, by now 10 years old, kept pace with copies of the plaque. Indeed, such was the longevity of the shield's popularity that Elkington was still advertising copies in the company's sale catalogue of 1904, and exhibiting it in its showrooms in Birmingham, London, Manchester, Liverpool and Glasgow. Always adept at publicizing its success, it claimed that given its purchase by 'the Government for the South Kensington Museum [it] has thus been adopted as a National Work of Art.'[7]

Elkington encouraged Morel-Ladeuil to repeat the success of the Milton Shield with a bicentennial tribute to John Bunyan's *Pilgrim's Progress* for the Paris Exposition Universelle of 1878. His Bunyan Shield, also in steel mounted with silver plaques, was never as popular. The Museum did not buy the original, ordering only a single copy in plain electroplate for the collection.[8] The original was still on display in Elkington's Birmingham showroom in 1904.

Electrotypes of the shield also made inspirational models in British factories. Few photographs of these workshops survive, but electrotypes of both the Milton and the Bunyan Shields appear on the back wall of Birmingham metalworkers Spital & Clark, in around 1910, alongside a range of plaster casts. Meanwhile, the engraving room of contemporaneous Sheffield silversmiths Walker & Hall displays a copy of the Milton Shield among dozens of models on the wall, a gallery of three-dimensional images influencing the creative output of generations of workers (28).

▶ (28)

The Engraving Room, Walker & Hall, Sheffield

Reproduced from a sale catalogue of *c*.1910 and showing model electrotypes and plaster casts on the wall, including at back right a copy of the Milton Shield

The original Milton Shield was one of the most expensive purchases the Museum made during the nineteenth century. More electrotypes of it were produced than for any other artwork.

It was a 'Modern Specimen', reproduced as an example of the best in contemporary design. The original was designed and sculpted by a great French artist for a pioneering British manufacturer, who reproduced it in large numbers and displayed it at international exhibitions, selling copies all over the globe. It was a truly modern artwork for an increasingly connected world.

# The Gates of Paradise

The electrotypes of the Gates of Paradise are copies of the doors made by Lorenzo Ghiberti (*c*.1378–1455) between 1425 and 1452 for the east portal of the Baptistery of Florence Cathedral (**29**). The original gilt bronze gates are widely regarded as one of the masterpieces of the Italian Renaissance. The copies were made for the Museum by Giovanni Franchi & Son in the 1860s from electroformed copper, which was then electrogilded to look like the originals (**30**).

Giovanni Franchi & Son was a copying firm, producing plaster figures, fictile ivories (small-scale plaster copies of ivory carvings) and electrotypes. Father and son were described in *The Art Journal* of 1866 as 'the only electrotypists who devote themselves to Fine Art'.[1]

When the Museum commissioned Giovanni Franchi to produce a copy of the Gates of Paradise, he requested that Luigi Stiatessi, the mould maker at the Uffizi in Florence, be responsible for taking the moulds.[2] Stiatessi had already made several other casts in the Museum's collection. The pre-eminence and skill of Italian mould makers was widely acknowledged, owing to the long history of casting and production of sculpture in Italy. Many of the English companies servicing the Museum's copying programme employed immigrant Italian mould makers.

The Tuscan government granted permission for the firm to take moulds of the doors in gutta-percha, a flexible tree resin similar to rubber that was imported from the Malay archipelago. Franchi predicted that this would take eight to nine months. However, a report in *The Builder* from 1870 describes how there was much 'popular indignation ... roused by the operatives', and Florentine opinion was divided as to whether the doors were being destroyed or prepared for exportation.[3] Seemingly as a result, the operation was suspended by order of the government. Instead, Franchi obtained permission to use a set of moulds produced at an earlier date. These moulds were widely considered

Giovanni Franchi & Son
(*fl*.1857–76)

Electrotype of the
Gates of Paradise

1867

Electrotype
767.5 × 473 cm
V&A: Repro.1867–44

Giovanni Franchi & Son
(*fl*.1857–76)

Panel from electrotype
of the Gates of Paradise

1867

Electrotype
V&A: Repro.1867–44

to have produced a more accurate copy of the original doors, since they replicated them as they appeared prior to further weathering.[4]

The plaster moulds were taken to Franchi's workshop in Clerkenwell, London, where they were used to create the electrotype copies. Transporting a large number of moulds across Europe was a complicated logistical process, and it was important that each mould was carefully numbered to ensure the correct layout of the panels and the accuracy of the copy.

To create the electrotype, the moulds were oiled to seal them and then lined with graphite to make them conductive. They were then suspended in a tank filled with a copper sulphate solution. Copper from the solution was then deposited into the moulds, particle by particle, by means of an electric current running through the tank.

Franchi agreed to provide the Tuscan government with a new set of moulds made from the electrotype copies, as the originals would have been discoloured by the materials used in the process. Each panel of the electrotype doors was produced individually (**31 & 32**) and each door was then constructed within a wood frame at the Museum. The firm sold metal copies of the complete doors for £950, but offered plaster casts for £60, and individual panels for between 10s. and £4 10s.

The teaching in the Museum of the 1860s focused greatly on the art of medieval and Renaissance Europe, and so obtaining a copy of the doors was a priority. The Gates of Paradise were the second set of doors designed by Ghiberti for the Florentine Baptistery. The first set depicted scenes from the New Testament, and had been completed between 1403 and 1424. The great success of these doors encouraged the ancient Calimala (Wool Merchants) Guild in Florence to commission Ghiberti to produce a second set of doors depicting scenes from the Old Testament. The original intention was to have 28 reliefs on the two later doors, but Ghiberti chose to simplify the scheme and have only ten panels, arranged in two columns of five, one column for each door. Each panel focuses on a significant event in the Old Testament, beginning in the upper left corner with the Creation and ending in the lower right corner with the story of Solomon.

These doors popularly became known as the Gates
of Paradise, and Michelangelo is said to have described
them as an 'opus divinum' (a divine work).[5]

# The reliefs are framed by 24 standing prophets and prophetesses, and 24 heads, including that of Ghiberti and his son Vittorio.

The electrotype copy was finally acquired in 1867,
the same year that the Convention for Promoting
Universally Reproductions of Works of Art for the
Benefit of Museums of All Countries was signed by
15 heads of state to encourage the procuring and
sharing of copies for the promotion of art education.

During the 1860s John Charles Robinson,
the Museum's first curator, had been leading a
sustained programme of reproducing and collecting
reproductions of Italian Renaissance art to complement
the Museum's growing collection of original works.
Franchi's copy of the Florentine Gates of Paradise
afforded an insight into Ghiberti's outstanding ability to
combine complex compositions with subtle gradations
of relief and an unprecedented use of perspective.[6]

The electrotyped doors were put on display in the
Museum's newly built South Courts until the Cast
Courts were built. There, according to *The Builder*,
they were shown with the Museum's 'unrivalled
collection of electrotypes, copies of famous works
of art in gold-plate, silver, bronze, and other metals,
of which the Museum has so good a right to boast.'
It encouraged 'those who would know the arts of
the sculptor, the founder, the modeller, the medallist,
and the goldsmith' to 'pay a speedy and a careful
visit to this scene of metallurgic triumph'.[7]

▶ (**32**)

Oronzio Lelli (*fl. c.*1860–1900)

Cast of a panel from Ghiberti's
first set of doors for the Baptistery
of Florence Cathedral, depicting
the Raising of Lazarus

1882

Plaster
61.5 × 51 cm
V&A: Repro.1882–23

1882-23

73

# The Pepys Cup

The Pepys Cup was one of the most impressive, complex and controversial objects reproduced as an electrotype (33). Copied by the Birmingham metalworking giants Elkington & Co., pioneers and patentees of electroplating, the cup became the focus of a dispute over the production of unlicensed copies.

The original cup was given to the Worshipful Company of Clothworkers by the naval administrator and diarist Samuel Pepys (1633–1703) and to this day remains one of the most important treasures in the Company's collection (34). The V&A owns no fewer than four electrotypes of the cup along with some of the copper type patterns created in its production. The type patterns were the first reproductions made during the process and from them future moulds could be made to save going back to the original, which may have been fragile or inaccessible. These patterns highlight the complex legal and ethical concerns surrounding the copying of works of art in the late nineteenth century.

Pepys was Master of the Clothworkers' Company from 1677 to 1678. To mark the beginning of his appointment as Master, Pepys presented the Company with several gifts to add to its plate collection: a rosewater dish, ewer and the cup, which became known as the Pepys Cup. The cup is topped with a ram, the emblem of the Clothworkers' Company, and decorated with elaborately pierced and chased ornament, making it a particularly beautiful and intricate example of English Baroque silver.

Nearly 200 years later, in 1873, the South Kensington Museum (as the V&A was then known) contacted the Clothworkers' Company to enquire about the possibility of commissioning Elkington to copy some of its notable plate collection. The Company confirmed that it was happy to participate, and put forward the Pepys Cup as one of the best pieces in its collection.

London livery companies were a prime target for electrotyping missions throughout the 1860s and 1870s as most had significant collections of historic silver.

Henry Cole had been quick to recognize the opportunities that electrotyping offered for the exposure of works of art that were otherwise hidden from the public. Copies enabled key pieces to be studied by a much wider audience, both within the Museum's own walls and further afield in regional museums across Britain. The scientist Robert Hunt had gone as far as to claim, 'The Electrotype will prove one of the most important auxiliary agents in the progressive advance of Art, in its ministrations to the improvement of Society.'[1] Negotiations with the owners of valuable historic treasures could be delicate, however, and some livery companies resisted the Museum's overtures.

Work on copying the Pepys Cup eventually began in July 1879. The cup was lent to the Museum, where moulds were taken before it was returned to the Clothworkers' Company. An 1886 letter from Elkington to the Museum notes that the cup had to be moulded in 29 separate pieces.[2] The level of detail replicated is extremely precise and captures the inscription on the base of the cup, documenting Pepys' gift to the Company. To prevent any possibility of confusion with the original, the hallmarks were deliberately obliterated on the copies and an oval badge was electroformed under the base, indicating that the cup was reproduced with the authority of the Science and Art Department that oversaw the Museum ( 35 ).

The collaboration with Elkington, which began in 1852 for a trial period of a year and lasted until the First World War, was a great success and had a profound influence on the development of the V&A's collections. Multiple copies of art works were lent or sold to museums and art schools around the world. Copies of the Pepys Cup were produced for museums in Sheffield, Bradford and Birmingham.

However, the relationship with Elkington was not without occasional tension. Matters took a sour turn, seven years after the first copies were made, when the cup was the subject of an exchange of letters between Elkington, the Museum and the Clothworkers' Company. In July 1886 a member of the Company, visiting the Folkestone Exhibition, observed that Elkington was offering copies of the Pepys Cup for sale at £30, with a ready-made example on display. The Company had been assured that no copies would be produced from the South Kensington Museum's type

▶ ( **34** )

Charles Thurston Thompson (1816–1868)

Specimens selected from the Special Exhibition of Works of Arts on Loan at the South Kensington Museum in 1862: a sepia-coloured photograph of the Pepys Cup, a silver cup and cover surmounted by a ram with inscription, mounted with a printed detail description and bound in an album with 33 other photographs

Commissioned by South Kensington Museum

1862

Albumen print
Album: 59 × 47.5 cm
V&A: 40306

No. 5,410. The "Pepys cup," a standing cup and cover of
silver, 23 inches high. It is covered with pierced flowers
and scrolls, the latter in four panels, wherein are a teasel, a
ram, a habbick, and a griffin. The cover is surmounted by
a ram. On the foot are the arms of Samuel Pepys,* his
initials, and his crest; and an inscription in Latin on the
cup records the gift in 1677. CLOTHWORKERS' COMPANY.

patterns without its express permission, and was therefore alarmed to learn that Elkington had apparently produced additional copies without its knowledge.

Owen Roberts, the Company's Clerk, wrote to the Museum to ask for an explanation. The Museum swiftly contacted Elkington & Co., which confirmed that five electrotype copies of the cup were in its possession. Elkington claimed these had been made in anticipation of orders for provincial museums, so as to speed up the delivery process and that they were not being offered for private sale. The Clothworkers' Company was unconvinced by this explanation and the Museum criticized this 'very serious and much to be regretted infraction of conditions'.[3] The Museum decided to purchase all the copies of the cup from Elkington. At the request of the Clothworkers' Company, the Museum also retrieved from Elkington all the type patterns for the Pepys Cup, to reduce the risk of any more unauthorized copies being made ( 36 ).

The Museum should have been guarding the type patterns already as they belonged to the Department of Science and Art. The clamour to copy had compromised protocols, an ongoing situation throughout the programme that came to a head in 1913. A Museum official wrote to the then director, Cecil Harcourt Smith (1859–1944), admitting that the system of confirming owners' permission for reproductions had never been properly established. 'These conditions we maintain strictly, although we have no means of really enforcing them.' He went on to claim that the Museum should 'maintain the fiction – even if it be nothing more' that Elkington's unshakeable habit of selling unauthorized copies was illegal.[4] The relationship with Elkington gradually dissolved after this period.

The four copies of the Pepys Cup in the V&A collection provide a remarkable testament to the miracle of electrotyping, which continues to impress and mystify visitors even now. The fraught correspondence between the three parties involved in their production, however, reminds us that today's questions over copyright, often associated with the latest developments in replication technologies, have a strong resonance with concerns expressed in the nineteenth century.

► ( 35 )

Department of Science and Art stamp on the base of the electrotype of the Pepys Cup

V&A: Repro.1879–6

► ( 36 )

Elkington & Co., Birmingham or London

Type pattern of the Pepys Cup

1879

Copper
17 × 22 × 9 cm
V&A: Repro.1879–6

# Mirror frame. Carved and gilt, Venetian, *c.*1690

◄ ( **37** )

Charles Thurston
Thompson (1816–1868)

*Mirror frame. Carved
and gilt, Venetian, c.1690*

1853

Albumen print
57.9 × 41 cm
V&A: 32639

Charles Thurston Thompson was among the world's
earliest museum photographers. Henry Cole, the first
director of the South Kensington Museum, appointed
him 'Official Photographer' in 1856, at which point he had
already been working for the Museum for several years.
Cole and Thurston Thompson knew each other from the
Great Exhibition in 1851, an event for which Cole had taken
a central organizational role and Thurston Thompson had
supervised the photographic arrangements. Here, in his
photograph of a mirror frame belonging to the collector
John Webb, his accidental reflection appears in the mirror
( **37** ). He had photographed the mirror when
documenting a loan exhibition of furniture at Gore House,
Kensington, in 1853. The photograph had to be taken
outside to ensure there was sufficient light and so part
of the Gore House garden can also be seen in the mirror.
Indeed, the only photographs of Thurston Thompson
currently known are those where his face, or an arm,
appear accidentally behind the camera, reflected in
mirrors being photographed.

Thurston Thompson had Cole's trust, and was
deployed in various ways by the Museum. As well as
photographing Museum objects and exhibitions, he was
also sent abroad to photograph architecture, such as the
Batalha monastery in Portugal and the Pórtico de la
Gloria at the Cathedral of Santiago de Compostela in
Spain. The Pórtico was of course also reproduced in
plaster for the Museum (see pp.46–51).

For the South Kensington Museum, photography in
particular epitomized the marriage of science and art it
so desired. Thurston Thompson was a leading practitioner
and was put into service to help share the collections with

the wider world. The first curator, John Charles Robinson, had noted in 1854 that, 'The photographic art is calculated to be of extraordinary utility in extending the influence of the collections such as this. Perhaps the most valuable characteristic of this extraordinary process being the perfect accuracy with which objects of art can be copied.' He went on to write that, 'Many most successful photographs have already been taken of objects in our collection … It is difficult indeed to fully estimate the probable effects of such reproduction in an instructional point of view, especially when it is borne in mind that copies may be multiplied to an indefinite extent.'[1]

In 1858 Thurston Thompson successfully negotiated permission to photograph the Raphael Cartoons at Hampton Court ( 38 ). They were then lent to the Museum from the Royal Collection in 1865, and remain at the Museum today. This was an ambitious project, which required purchase of a special outsize lens and camera. As with the mirror, the photography had to be done outdoors, and so arrangements were made to bring the cartoons carefully out of a window at Hampton Court, one by one. The Museum used the resulting photographs not just as reference images but also as active working documents. In 1865 a set of these prints was annotated by Richard Redgrave, then Inspector-General of the Government School of Design, to show the physical condition of the cartoons in minutely plotted detail. This practice of annotating photographs of Museum objects with conservation information continues in much the same way today. Some of the negatives from this project still survive, and although the prints were cropped to the edge of each cartoon, in the negatives details of the building of Hampton Court are visible in the background.

From the beginning of his Museum career, Thurston Thompson was assisted in his photographic work by members of the Royal Engineers. Unusually, the sappers, as they were called, were billeted at the Museum and not only assisted with the construction of new buildings in the Museum but also acted as warders and general assistants in many practical areas of Museum work. Soon after his appointment, it was decided that Thurston Thompson would formally train several Royal Engineers for a year in photography, with successful individuals gaining a certificate at the end of the training. It was recognized early on that photography was a useful tool in military surveys, and for copying maps. Many Royal Engineers who had been trained at the Museum went on to develop significant bodies of photographic work. From the Royal Engineers who photographed the Canada/United States border as part of a boundary survey in 1858–62 to the photographers of the Palestine Exploration Fund, the influence of Thurston Thompson's training was wide, and is still being revealed.

Although it cannot always be stated with certainty that any Royal Engineer trained in photography had been taught at South Kensington, it seems possible that Ludovico Wolfgang Hart, who photographed in Syria, Egypt and Nubia in the 1860s, was indeed trained by Thurston Thompson, as was Arthur Vipond, who accompanied the border commission in British Columbia. Sergeant Mack and Corporals Milliken, Church and Spackman were sappers known to have worked with Thurston Thompson in the Museum's photographic studio and to have taken photographs themselves.

Thurston Thompson's picture of the mirror frame is one of the earliest object photographs in the collection. It has the added significance of giving us a glimpse of a man who had a profound influence on the development of museum photography.

▶ (**38**)

Charles Thurston Thompson
(1816–1868)

Raphael Cartoon,
*Elymas struck with Blindness*

1858

Albumen print
62 × 79.8 cm
V&A: 76601

PHOTOGRAPH OF

# Brown satin jacket

◂ ( **39** )

Isabel Agnes Cowper
(1826–1911)

*Brown satin jacket*
English, 17th century

1873

Albumen print from wet
collodion on glass negative
58.8 × 37 cm
V&A: 74934B

When Charles Thurston Thompson died unexpectedly in 1868, his sister Isabel Agnes Cowper took charge of the Photographic Studio, remaining in post until 1891. This photograph of a seventeenth-century doublet comes from a set she took that documented objects in the Loan Exhibition of Art Needlework that held at the Museum in 1873 ( **39** ).

Photography does not require physical contact with objects, enabling reproductions of objects too fragile to be cast or electrotyped. This allowed images of textiles, ceramics and glass to be reproduced and shared around the world. By producing this photograph in a large format, Cowper was able to show the intricate stitches. Copies of the photographs were circulated to other institutions, as both the exhibition and the photographs were created with the aim of inspiring needleworkers. The School of Art Needlework (now the Royal School of Needlework), situated close to the Museum, had opened the previous year. The aim of this institution was to revive the art of decorative embroidery, and so the exhibition and resulting photographs would have been studied closely by its students.

## Having a female 'Official Photographer' was highly unusual for the period.

It is clear that due to her gender and family responsibilities, Cowper's ability to travel abroad in the way that Thurston Thompson had done was limited. It had been thought previously that Cowper may not have taken the images herself, but recent research has shown that she entered her photographs in exhibitions, and her

▶ (**40**)

Isabel Agnes Cowper
(1826–1911)

*The Crucified Christ*,
attributed to Giovanni
Pisano

1871

Glass plate negative
25.5 × 20.2 cm
V&A: 9359

▶ (**41**)

Isabel Agnes Cowper
(1826–1911)

Cast of the head of
Michelangelo's *David*

1881

Albumen print
33 × 26.7 cm
V&A: 80552

signature or initials are sometimes visible in the corner of the surviving glass plate negatives ( **40** ). It is clear she was a working photographer.

Cowper did not limit her output to what might have been regarded then as traditionally feminine subjects, such as needlework, as many of her photographs document machinery and apparatus in the Science collections, electrotypes and the architectural interiors of the growing Museum. These needlework photographs, however, showcase her precision as a photographer and demonstrate the richness of depth and detail possible with the collodion process at this date. Introduced in 1851 by F. Scott Archer, the collodion process produced negatives on glass rather than on paper, which gave a higher resolution of detail.

Photographing copies, as opposed to original works, was commonplace in the Museum during the nineteenth century. Cowper photographed many electrotypes purchased by the Museum from Elkington & Co., and her images of casts span everything from the spectacular Trajan's Column, shown being erected in the Cast Courts, to smaller works used as drawing exercises by the National Art Training School, such as a reduced-size copy of the head of Michelangelo's *David* ( **41** ).

The School, which later evolved to become the Royal College of Art, was based inside the South Kensington Museum for many decades. It had a strict and prescriptive syllabus, which became known as the South Kensington System, in which drawing from casts played a large role. Photographers sometimes favoured photographing casts over original sculptures in bronze or marble, as the matt surface of plaster allowed greater control of the lighting effects and tonal range.

Thurston Thompson had died before completing his photography of the Pórtico de la Gloria from Santiago de Compostela. His photographs were taken for a book intended to document visually every section of the carving. In order that the book could be published, Cowper filled the missing sections by photographing the cast of the Pórtico in the Cast Courts. Her work is uncredited in the book.

1632.—89.

The Leaning Obelisk or Idol in the Ruins of Quirigua.
Made from moulds taken on the spot by A. P. Maudslay, Esq.
1889–82.

# Cast of leaning obelisk or idol in the ruins of Quiriguá

◄ ( **42** )

Alfred Percival Maudslay
(1850–1931)

*Cast of leaning obelisk or idol
in the ruins of Quiriguá*

*c*. 1889

Albumen print from gelatin
dry-plate negative
42.5 × 24.3 cm
V&A: PH.1632–1889

Casting, electrotyping, photography and other copying technologies were often used as mutually supporting methods of reproduction. Three-dimensional copies in museums were displayed with photographs of the copied object, included to show the site-specific context of the original. Photography, as the cheapest, quickest and most portable reproduction method, was often used as an intermediary when choosing which objects, features and details merited reproduction in three dimensions.

Photographs were also used as reference objects for the assembly of large casts. These tended to be cast in many sections, transported in pieces, and were then put together like a jigsaw puzzle at the final destination, quite possibly by people who had never seen the original work. Photographs of the original could be sent with the casts in order to get the arrangement of cast pieces correct.

A cast of Mayan carving from Quiriguá in Guatemala, was made by the Italian cast maker Lorenzo Giuntini (1844/5–1920) for the explorer and archaeologist Alfred Percival Maudslay (1850–1931) ( **42** ). Giuntini was responsible for several other casts in the Cast Courts, and at one time worked for D. Brucciani & Co., a key plaster modelling firm with close links to the South Kensington Museum (as the V&A was then known).

Also accompanying Maudslay in Guatemala was Gorgonio Lopez, who took papier mâché 'squeezes' (moulds or copies) of carved reliefs. This was a quicker and lighter three-dimensional copying technique than casting, although it picked up less detail than plaster. Maudslay was particularly interested in attempting to decipher the Mayan written language carved onto these monuments, and used all the most current reproduction techniques available to him to record examples in the field.

As well as commissioning and photographing casts, Maudslay took photographs at key sites, making use of the recently invented dry-plate photography ( **43** ). This more portable developing technique extended the range of photographers, allowing them to take images in environments where previously it had been too difficult. Maudslay gave his casts, squeezes, photographs and negatives to the South Kensington Museum in the 1880s, but apart from a few photographs, the collection is now held by the British Museum, having been transferred there in the early twentieth century.

The cast of the obelisk is shown on display in the Cast Courts, and nearby in the photograph can be seen an electrotype of an eleventh-century German chandelier and a painted copy of a Gobelins tapestry.

The presence of these Mayan casts highlights how the Courts were once more varied than they are today, and included a much broader range of casts and other copies showcasing more styles, areas and epochs.

This wider mix, coupled with the inclusion in the original Courts of a 4-metre long diagram comparing the heights of buildings around the world, demonstrates the importance placed on contrasting global objects and styles as part of the Museum's educational programme.

This international approach was a prevailing sentiment within the Museum during Henry Cole's era, but by the early twentieth century it was felt that the Cast Courts should instead demonstrate the best examples of a generally much narrower canon of Romanesque, Gothic and Renaissance art. Many casts were therefore given to other museums or, in some cases, destroyed. The Indian casts, which were once such a spectacular feature of the Courts, were transferred to the Imperial Institute, now Imperial College, and subsequently destroyed. The classical casts, gathered for the Museum by Walter Copeland Perry in the 1880s, and Maudslay's Mayan casts were among those transferred to the British Museum in the 1930s. Some of the Middle Eastern casts were also destroyed or transferred.

The National Art Library in the Museum began collecting photographs in the 1850s, and made them available to the public in the Reading Room. The Library built up a vast collection of photographs of places, architecture and artworks from around the world, initially to provide reference images for students and designers. While Maudslay's casts and negatives were transferred, some of his photographs remained in the Library for comparison and inspiration.

▶ ( **43** )

Alfred Percival Maudslay
(1850–1931)

Temple A, Menché,
Guatemala

*c.*1880–6

Albumen print from gelatin
dry-plate negative
21 × 16.5 cm
V&A: PH.631–1886

# Techniques and Conservation

# Plaster casting

Moulding and casting techniques developed thousands of years ago. Since then casting methods have become more sophisticated, but the principle of cast making remains the same. The development of techniques such as 3D imaging, milling and printing have extended the methods available for creating three-dimensional reproductions.

A cast is an impression, the reproduction of a form, made by means of a mould that takes information directly from the surface of an original. The reproduction has the potential to be virtually identical in shape to the original, depending on the skill of the mould maker, but the material is generally gypsum plaster.

Two types of mould can be used to create the negative impression of the original: flexible or rigid. During the nineteenth century, flexible moulds were commonly made of gelatin, clay, wax, gutta-percha (a natural tree resin imported from the Malay archipelago) or paper. Rigid moulds, known as piece-moulds, were generally made of plaster, in pieces that interlock. Many of the casts in the V&A's Cast Courts will have been made by a combination of both types.

The complexity of the original influences the choice of material for the mould and its construction. The mould-maker has to consider the form of the original initially, and then design the safest and most efficient way to cast it without trapping the mould in undercuts or recesses, such as curls of hair or folds of drapery. The technique used must also avoid damaging the original or the mould itself. A flexible mould can be made in a small number of sections, while a plaster piece-mould will be made up of many parts, sometimes numbering into the hundreds, depending on the size and complexity of the original. The mould taken from Michelangelo's statue of Giuliano de' Medici, for example, comprised over 200 pieces.

The pieces are made individually to fit the surface of the original and each other. They surround the object like a three-dimensional jigsaw puzzle and are held together in a jacket, known as a mother-mould. Moulds for reliefs

D. Brucciani & Co., London
(*fl.*1851–1915)

Mould for casting a head
of Moses

Before 1889

Plaster
V&A: A.2–2018

are normally shallow, and may consist of just one piece, whereas those for more three-dimensional forms may completely surround the void to be filled. A release agent, such as fat or wax, is applied to the original and the mould, to protect them and to ease the process.

# Plaster is an ideal material for casting: it spreads easily across different types of surfaces when wet, it thickens in a short but not too rapid time, and maps precisely the surface once it has set.

Liquid plaster is poured into the mould, which is then rotated carefully to ensure the plaster fills all the detailing. It expands slightly while setting, and fills even fine crevices. After the plaster has hardened sufficiently, the cast is carefully released from the mould. Casts may be solid or hollow, depending on the scale or the preference of the cast maker, and will often contain strengtheners within the mixture, such as hessian or hair, or metal armatures. For highly complex objects moulds are made of different sections. Once cast, the different sections are joined together to build up the whole.

On release from the mould, some finishing is necessary. Seam lines on the surface may be smoothed, and the plaster soaked or coated to make it more durable. During the nineteenth century this could be a fundamental aspect of the process, and cast makers had their own recipes. Finally, colour could be applied to the surface.

# Electrotyping

◄ ( **45** )

'Plating' at Elkington's factory in Newhall Street, Birmingham

*The Illustrated Exhibitor*, 1852, p.296
NAL PP.8.QDW

◄ ( **46** )

Copper type patterns, V&A

An electrotype is a copy made when metal is deposited, using an electrical charge, into a mould taken from another object. The process is largely the same now as it was during the nineteenth century, although the materials used vary slightly.

To make the mould today, a soft, almost liquid silicon rubber is pressed onto the surface of the original. During the nineteenth century materials such as wax, plaster and gutta-percha (a tree resin from the Malay archipelago) were used instead. On cooling the rubber sets and hardens to create an accurate impression of the surface of the original. The mould is flexible enough to be able to be released from an object with pronounced decoration without breaking.

The mould is then painted with a metallic solution (usually silver) to help it conduct electricity (nineteenth-century factories used graphite, known then as plumbago, a form of coal). Copper wires are attached to the surface of the mould and it is suspended in a vat filled with copper sulphate. A piece of copper is also suspended in the vat in case the copper content in the solution runs out during the process. An electrical current is switched on and passed through the solution. Positively charged copper ions are drawn towards the negatively charged mould, plating it with copper ( **45** ).

When enough copper is deposited onto the mould to ensure that the copy will be strong enough to support its own weight, the mould is removed from the vat and the copper form is removed from the mould. Additional copies can be made from this first electroform without having to re-mould the original. This is known as a 'type pattern' ( **46** ).

The edges of the electroform are trimmed and tidied up using files. If desired, the copper electrotype can be decorated by immersing it into another bath and either electroplating it to look like silver, or electrogilding it to look like gold. The Museum's electrotypes were marked with a stamp to distinguish them from the originals and show they had been made under licence.

# Plaster casts

◄ ( 47 )

Ultraviolet light reveals
information about the
condition of the coatings:
the dark areas on this lion's
head, from the Nicola
Pisano pulpit, Pisa,
show that there is no
longer any coating,
leaving the surface porous

V&A: Repro.1864–83
Photograph: Sofia Marques
© Victoria and Albert Museum,
London

◄ ( 48 )

Iron bars, added during
the casting of panels from
Trajan's Column, have
rusted over time and
expanded. Where they
are very close to the
surface, the expansion
has caused the plaster to
crack and flake off

V&A: Repro.1864–128
Photograph: Leo Crowther
© Victoria and Albert Museum,
London

Perhaps due to its association with buildings, or because casts often take on the form, appearance and scale of strong materials, plaster tends to be perceived as a robust material. It is, however, fragile, brittle and porous. To counteract this, methods have evolved to give strength and durability to plaster casts, with varying degrees of success.

When considering the conservation of casts, the constituent materials and the influence of time should be understood, as they lead to an array of variables. All *formatori*, or cast makers, had their own recipes and methods that aimed to overcome this fragility: casts in a collection will not be uniform, and each difference affects how a cast ages, and what its conservation needs are. Definition of the different factors requires visual examination with magnification and ultraviolet light sources, aided by solvent tests and scientific analyses ( 47 ).

Plaster casts are made from the mineral gypsum, which has been burned to drive off water of crystallization, creating a powder that reacts with water. The reaction causes the formation of interlocking needle-like crystals, which produce a solid but porous mass.

The structure of the plaster itself is affected by the proportion of water used in the mixing, and whether or not accelerators or retardants were added by the *formatore*. While casts may be made solid, one of the properties of plaster is that a relatively thin layer, when set, will support itself, allowing hollow structures to be created. To make it durable, the resulting lightweight structure would need strengtheners, such as hessian or hair, added to the plaster mix, or armatures added during the build-up of layers. Historically, wood or iron rods have been used ( 48 ). The construction of the finished piece may also play a role – a large or complex piece would be cast in separate parts. Which, on installation would be joined together with more plaster as required, with the introduction of further support structures in metal or wood ( 49 ).

These structural materials may introduce
weakness over time, due to differential expansion
and contraction in response to the environment,
as well as corrosion of metal, creating cracks
or even causing loss in the plaster.

When poured into a mould, the resulting cast
will have a smooth surface that belies the degree
of porosity. Left untreated, the plaster would absorb
moisture and dirt, rapidly discolouring and becoming
susceptible to abrasion. How to create a hardened
surface has been a concern of generations of *formatori*,
with the hunt for a solution resulting in innumerable
recipes for coatings.

Not all recipes
were written down.
Among those published,
materials such as animal
glue, linseed oil, milk,
tree resins, waxes and
soaps were recommended,
either on their own or
in mixtures.

In some cases, the coatings were selected to preserve
the whiteness, while in others pigments have been
added to reproduce the colour of the originals.
In many cases, the materials used can effectively
protect the surfaces for decades, but will slowly break
down, becoming yellowed and eroded, resulting in
patchy and absorbent surfaces. In the past this has
resulted in additional coatings or paint being applied,
adding further complexity to the conservator's
evaluation when assessing casts for condition.

▲ ( **49** )

The cast of the synagogue
from Toledo, Spain, was
made in panels and joined
together in situ in the
gallery. In some joints,
extra plaster was added
and reworked with
a serrated tool. Also visible
are two round raised areas
of plaster, where iron
screws used in the
construction have rusted
and expanded

V&A: Repro.1871–60

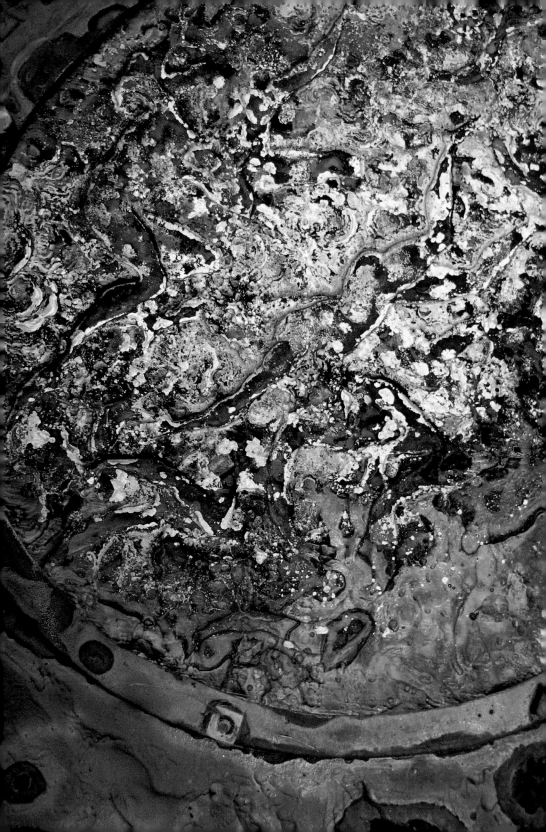

# Electrotypes

Most electrotypes are copper, either plain or plated with another metal, usually silver or gold. Sometimes the copper is chemically treated to change its colour to mimic bronze, steel, pewter or oxidized silver. This chemical process can produce a surface that looks similar to tarnish. The conservator must be careful to ascertain what is the original surface of the electrotype, and what is in fact tarnish that should be removed.

This need to distinguish the original surface from later tarnish is made slightly more complicated by the fact that some electrotypes, such as the Milton Shield, were sold in several different finishes, according to budget and taste ( **50** ). Some of these finishes differed radically from the appearance of the original object. The V&A's electrotypes of the shield were 'Bronze, silver and oxydised with bands gilt where damascened in the original A. quality.'[1]

Others were sold as plain electroplate, or even gilded. Close examination during treatment revealed that the 'bronzed' parts of the shield were actually electroplated in silver, and then patinated or 'oxidized' darker, although oxidized is a misleading term as the process actually uses sulphur, which combines with silver to produce the dark surface.

Electrotypes that have been plated and oxidized can show evidence of delamination, where the deliberately oxidized surface has further deteriorated, and the resulting thick layer of silver tarnish peels away, leaving a matt silver surface. Treatment of electrotypes therefore has to be undertaken with care. Mechanical removal of the tarnish using a silver cloth and chalk rubber is followed by rinsing the affected areas with a solvent. The electrotype is then lacquered in order to reduce further tarnishing. The lacquer is easy to remove, since wherever possible all conservation treatment should be reversible. Once treated, metals should ideally be kept in low humidity, as the presence of water in the air can cause or speed up tarnishing.

# Notes
# and
# Bibliography

# Notes

## Introduction

1   Conway 1882, pp.21–3.

2   *The Builder*, October 1873.

## Michelangelo's *David*

1   Fifth Report of the Department of Science and Art, p.70. 'Donations to the Museum of Art in 1857, H.R.H. the Grand Duke of Tuscany – cast of statue of Michael Angelo's *David* at Florence.'

2   The original marble figure of *David* has been displayed at the Galleria dell'Accademia (Accademia Gallery) in Florence since 1873.

3   There are still traces of plaster on the sling strap on the original marble left by Papi's casting process. Falletti 1997, p.61.

4   See Cast Courts blog on the V&A website for further details: www.vam.ac.uk.

5   In *The Art Journal*, new series, 1 January 1857, vol. 3, p.162, the royal gift is referred to in 'Minor Topics of the Month' where it is mentioned that 'M. Brucciani, of Little Russell Street, Covent Garden, having a mould is able to furnish casts of the bust and other portions of this remarkable specimen of the Florentine school.'

## Trajan's Column

1   V&A Archive, ED84/36. Precis of the Board Minutes of the Science and Art Department. Vols 2 and 3, 13 July 1872.

2   V&A Archive, ED84/15. Specification of works for the completion of the carcase of the new South-East Court and general conditions, 21 July 1870.

3   'The South Kensington Museum: The New Architectural Court', *The Art Journal*, 1873, vol. 7, p.27.

4   V&A Archive, MA/2/T6. Nominal File: Trajan's Column.

5   Mosley 1964, p.31.

6   Mosley 1964, p.33.

## The Pórtico de la Gloria

1   'A Glory to the Museum: the Casting of the Pórtico de la Gloria', V&A Album 1, 1982, pp.101–8.

2   Ana Laborde Marqueze and Francisco Prado Vilar, 'La restauración del Pórtico de la Gloria en la Catedral de Santiago de Compostela', *Concha Cirujano*, 2012, no. 6, pp.183–95.

3   'La culminación de la catedral románica: El maestro Mateo y la escenografía de la Gloria y el Reino' in Valle Pérez (ed.) 2013, pp.989–1018.

4   V&A Archive, MA/3/16. Robinson's Reports Box, pp.17, 19.

5   El Pórtico de la Gloria en la Inglaterra Victoriana: La invención de una obra maestra, Ministry of Culture – National Museum of Pilgrimages, Santiago de Compostela, 1991, p.94.

6   V&A Archive, MA/3/17. Robinson's Reports Box, pp.75–7.

7   Enrique Fernández Castiñeiras, 'Pintores neoclásicos compostelanos', *ADAXE*, 1987, no. 3, pp.41–62.

8   Conservation Reports. Sculpture Conservation Archive & Analysis Report, 201–18, pp.17–52-LB-VR Santiago de Compostela porch – Repro.1866–50, Lucia Burgio and Valentina Risdonne, Science Section, Conservation Department.

9   Reports to Henry Cole on the plaster cast of the Pórtico della Gloria, Santiago. NAL: 86.YY.70.

## Islamic Ornament

1   Report by Ralph Wornum, then Keeper of the Cast Collection and Professor of Ornament, in First Report 1853, p.289.

2   V&A: Repro.1883–215 to 264. On the V&A's collecting of material from Islamic Spain, in particular the Alhambra, see Rosser-Owen 2011.

3   *Guide to the Collections of the South Kensington Museum*, London 1888, p.4.

4   V&A Archive, MA/1/C1212.
    On Chester's textile collecting activities,
    see Persson 2010.

5   V&A Archive, MA/1/L257.

6   Stanley Lane-Poole, *The Art of the Saracens
    in Egypt*, London 1886, pp.9–16.

7   An observation made in 1900, quoted in
    Williams 2008, p.173, without a reference.
    He also said: 'It is, indeed, in the buildings
    of the Sultan Kaït Bey [*sic*] that both the
    pure arabesque and the finest geometrical
    ornament are seen in their perfection'.
    Lane-Poole 1886, p.94.

8   Wornum, in First Report 1853, p.290.

9   V&A: E.3644 to 4084–1938. Owen Jones
    based the 'Arabian' plates of *The Grammar
    of Ornament* closely on the drawings in
    Wild's sketchbooks.

10  On which see the publications by
    Mercedes Volait.

11  See Moya Carey and Mercedes Volait,
    'Framing "Islamic Art" for aesthetic
    interiors: revisiting the 1878 Paris
    exhibition', *International Journal of Islamic
    Architecture*, forthcoming.

12  V&A Archive, MA/1/S180: 'Memorandum
    on the Egypto-Arabian Collection in the
    Paris Exhibition 1878' (1882).

### The Milton Shield

1   George Wallis, quoted in Sandhurst
    and Mueller 1876, p.158.

2   V&A Search the Collections,
    V&A: 546–1868.

3   *The Art Journal Illustrated Catalogue
    of the Universal Exhibition*, London,
    1868, p.217.

4   *The Times*, 4 September 1867.

5   V&A Search the Collections,
    V&A: Repro.138–1868.

6   Patterson 2011. See also V&A Search
    the Collections, V&A: Repro.4–1879.

7   Elkington & Co. Ltd, Sale Catalogue,
    Birmingham, 1904, p.183.

8   V&A Search the Collections,
    V&A: Repro.3–1879.

### The Gates of Paradise

1   'Electro-Metallurgy', *The Art Journal*, 1866,
    vol. 5, p.287.

2   V&A Archive, MA/1/F1178. Moulding of the
    Ghiberti Gates of Florence and the Perseus
    of Cellini, 6 February 1864.

3   'The Ghiberti-Gates in the South
    Kensington Museum', *The Builder*, 1870,
    pp.58–9.

4   Ibid.

5   Radke 2007.

6   'The Ghiberti-Gates in the South
    Kensington Museum', *The Builder*, 1870,
    pp.58–9.

7   Ibid.

### The Pepys Cup

1   Robert Hunt, 'On the Application of
    Science on the Fine and Useful Arts: The
    Electrotype', *The Art Union*, 1 April 1848.

2   Reproduction of College and Corporation
    Plate, volume of transcribed
    correspondence from the V&A Archive in
    the Metalwork Section Library of the V&A,
    1873–87, pp.47a–f.

3   Ibid.

4   V&A Archives, MA/1/E468/15 –
    1915/3703M. Elkington & Co. Files, Memo
    from H.P. Mitchell to Cecil Harcourt Smith,
    undated.

### Mirror frame, carved and gilt, Venetian, *c.*1690

1   John Charles Robinson, 'Documents
    relating to Administration of Museum',
    Appendix G to First Report of Department
    of Science and Art, 1 January 1854, p.231.

### Conservation: Electrotypes

1   *Private Collections*, Science and
    Art Department of the Committee
    of Council on Education, South Kensington
    Museum, London, 1870, p.56.

# Bibliography

Archive sources

J.C. Robinson, Official Reports, Museum of Art 1852–1857, V&A Archive

Primary sources

*Convention for Promoting Universally, Reproductions of Works of Art for the Benefit of Museums of All Countries*, Paris, 1867, National Art Library: MSL/1921/1153-1162

Conway 1882
Moncure Daniel Conway, *Travels in South Kensington with Notes on Decorative Art and Architecture in England* (London, 1882)

Sandhurst and Muelle 1876r
Phillip T. Sandhurst and A. M. J Mueller, *The Great Centennial Exhibition Critically Described and Illustrated* (Philadelphia, 1876)

Smee 1840
Alfred Smee, *Elements of Electro-Metallurgy* (London, 1840)

*The Art Journal Illustrated Catalogue of the Universal Exhibition* (London, 1868)

Secondary sources

Baker and Richardson 1997
Malcolm Baker and Brenda Richardson (eds), *A Grand Design: The Art of the Victoria and Albert Museum* (New York, 1997)

Bernardini et al. 1989
Luisella Bernardini et al. (eds), *La scultura italiana dal XV al XX secolo nei calchi della Gipsoteca*, exh. cat., Istituto Statale d'Arte, Florence, 1989

Bryant 2011
Julius Bryant (ed.), *Art and Design For All: The Victoria and Albert Museum* (London, 2011)

Burton 1999
Anthony Burton, *Vision and Accident: The Story of the Victoria and Albert Museum* (London, 1999)

*Copia e invención* 2013
'The Conservation of the Cast Courts at the Victoria and Albert Museum: The Cast of the Pórtico de la Gloria', *Copia e invención*, conference proceedings, Museo Nacional de Escultura, Spain, 2013, pp.227–42

Edwards and Morton, 2015
Elizabeth Edwards and Christopher Morton (eds), *Photographs, Museums, Collections: Between Art and Information* (London, 2015)

Falletti 1997
Franca Falletti (ed.), *The Place for David, Accademia, Michelangelo, the Nineteenth Century, A Series of Studies* (Livorno, 1997)

Grant and Patterson 2019
Alistair Grant and Angus Patterson, *The Museum and the Factory: The V&A, Elkington and the Electrical Revolution* (London, 2019)

Lederman 2017
E. Lederman, 'Isabel Agnes Cowper: Official Photographer at the V&A Museum' in J. Ashton (ed.), *Feminism and Museums: Intervention, Disruption and Change*, (Edinburgh, 2017), vol. 2, pp.560–600

Lending 2017
Mari Lending, *Plaster Monuments: Architecture and the Power of Reproduction* (New Jersey, 2017)

Mills 1990
John Mills, *The Technique of Casting for Sculpture* (London, 1990)

Mosley 1964
James Mosley, *Trajan Revived* (Birmingham, 1964)

Patterson 2011
Angus Patterson, 'The Pompeian Lady Plaque', *The Journal of the Antique Metalware Society*, 2011, vol. 19, pp.76–81

Patterson 2012
Angus Patterson, 'The Perfect Marriage of Art
and Industry: Elkingtons and the South
Kensington Museum's Electrotype Collection',
*The Journal of the Antique Metalware Society*,
2012, vol. 20, pp.56–77

Persson 2010
Helen Persson, 'Collecting Egypt: the Textile
Collection of the Victoria and Albert Museum',
*Journal of the History of Collections*, 2010,
pp.1–11

Physick 1975
John Physick, *Photography and the South
Kensington Museum* (London, 1975)

Physick 1982
John Physick, *The Victoria and Albert Museum:
The History of its Building* (London, 1982)

Radke 2007
Gary M. Radke (ed.), *The Gates of Paradise:
Lorenzo Ghiberti's Renaissance Masterpiece*
(London, 2007)

Robertson 1978
David Robertson, *Sir Charles Eastlake and
The Victorian Art World* (New Jersey, 1978)

Rosser-Owen 2011
Mariam Rosser-Owen, 'Collecting the Alhambra:
Owen Jones and Islamic Spain at the South
Kensington Museum' in Juan Calatrav (ed.), *Owen
Jones y la Alhambra* (Granada, 2011), pp.159–68

Shields 2015
Duncan Shields, 'Multiple Collections and Fluid
Meanings: Alfred Maudslay's Archaeological
Photographs at the British Museum' in Elizabeth
Edwards and Christopher Morton (eds),
*Photographs, Museums, Collections: Between
Art and Information* (London, 2015)

Trusted 2010
Marjorie Trusted, '"The Question of Casts" –
Collecting and Later Reassessment of the
Cast Collections at South Kensington' (with
D. Bilbey) in Rune Frederiksen and Eckart
Marchand (eds), *Plaster Casts: Making, Displaying
and Collecting from Classical Antiquity to the
Present* (Berlin and New York, 2010), pp.465–83

Trusted 2012
Marjorie Trusted, 'Reproduction as Spectacle,
Education and Inspiration' in Charlotte
Schreiter (ed.), *Gipsabgüsse und Antike
Skulpturen, Präsentation und Kontext*
(Berlin, 2012), pp.355–71

Trusted 2016
Marjorie Trusted, 'The Making and Meaning
of Plaster Casts in the Nineteenth Century.
Their Future in the Twenty-First Century'
in Christina Haak and Miguel Helfrich (eds),
*Casting. A way to embrace the digital age in
analogue fashion?: A symposium on the
Gipsformerei of the Staatlichen Museen zu
Berlin*, arthistoricum.net, 2016

Trusted 2017
Marjorie Trusted, 'Medieval Scandinavia and
Victorian South Kensington' in Sara Ayres and
Elettra Carbone (eds), *Sculpture and the Nordic
Region* (London, 2017), pp.102–17

Volait 1998
Mercedes Volait, *L'Egypte d'un architecte:
Ambroise Baudry, 1838–1906* (Paris, 1998)

Volait 2009
Mercedes Volait, *Fous du Caire; excentriques,
architectes et amateurs d'art en Egypte,
1863–1914* (Montpellier, 2009)

Volait 2012
Mercedes Volait, *Maisons de France au Caire:
le remploi de grands décors mamelouks et
ottomans dans une architecture modern*
(Paris, 2012)

von Gaertringen 2012
Hans G. Hiller von Gaertringen, *Masterpieces
of the Gipsformerei, Art manufactory of the
Staatliche Museen zu Berlin since 1819*
(Munich, 2012)

Wager 1952
Victor H. Wager, *Plaster Casting for the Student
Sculptor* (London, 1952)

Williams 2008
Caroline Williams, *Islamic Monuments in Cairo:
the Practical Guide* (Cairo and New York, 2008)

# Acknowledgements

The editors are particularly grateful to the chapter authors for providing such interesting and informative object studies, the breadth of topics reflecting the wide-ranging research and conservation of historic copies that takes place at the V&A.

The Museum would like to extend special thanks to those who have generously supported the Cast Courts redevelopment project: Garfield Weston Foundation, Ruddock Foundation for the Arts, N. Sethia Foundation, American Friends of the V&A, American Express, DCMS/Wolfson Museums and Galleries Improvement Fund, The Sarikhani Collection, The Lord Leonard and Lady Estelle Wolfson Foundation, Henry Moore Foundation, Peri Charitable Foundation, The Salomon Oppenheimer Philanthropic Foundation, Patricia Wengraf Ltd, Friends of Heritage Preservation, Allchurches Trust, Sam Fogg, Nicholas and Judith Goodison's Charitable Settlement, The Pilgrim Trust and many other supporters.

The Museum has also worked closely with key practitioners in the research and conservation of historic copies and in the production of modern copies and is particularly grateful to Adam Lowe and The Factum Foundation, Roger Michel and Alexy Karenowska (The Institute for Digital Archaeology), Alastair Hamer and Karleung Wai (RapidForm/Royal College of Art), Alex Ziff (3D Compare), Jon Beck (ScanTheWorld), Richard Lewis (BJS Company Ltd.), Henry H. Arnhold, Fundación Barrié de la Maza, Instituto de Patrimonio Cultural Español (IPCE) and The Radcliffe Trust.

Key V&A colleagues who have contributed both to the Cast Courts Project and to the production of this book include: Anais Aguerre, Soraya Alcalà, Eric Bates, Sarah Beattie, Mark Blackaller, Antonia Boström, Julius Bryant, Lucia Burgio, Ana Cabrera, Moya Carey, Sau Fong Chan, Tao Chang, Rachel Church, Jasmine Clark, Matthew Clarke, Brendan Cormier, Leo Crowther, Evelyn Curtin, Cathy Dabrowski, Richard Davis, Jo Dickinson, Doug Dodds, Richard Edgcumbe, Emma Edwards, Erik Ehrsson, George Eksts, Hanne Faurby, Steve Firth, Simon Goss, Catriona Gourlay, Melissa Hamnett, Sarah Healey-Dilkes, Diana Heath, Coralie Hepburn, Sergio Merida Hernandez, Tristram Hunt, Steve Hyde, Ken Jackson, Phil James, Chloe Johnson, Clare Johnson, Corinne Jones, Joanna Jones, Peter Kelleher, Chloe Kellow, Brenda Keneghan, Whitney Kerr-Lewis, Jane Lawson, Erika Lederman, Jordan Lewis, Reino Liefkes, Sofia Marques, Christopher Marsden, Asha McLoughlin, Arianna Francescutto Miro, Anthony Misquitta, Andrew Monks, Kate Morais, Nika Narkeviciute, Joanna Norman, Richard Palmer, Lucie Pieri, Kati Price, Jevgenija Ravcova, Paul Robins, Valentina Risdonne, Anthony Ryan, Graham Saffill, Sophie Sheldrake, Bryony Shepherd, Bill Sherman, Christine Smith, Nicholas Smith, Chloe Stewart, Reena Suleman, Danielle Thom, Livia Turnbull, Melanie Vandenbrouck, Amanda Ward, Thomas Waring, Marta Weiss, Joanna Whalley, Tom Windross and Catherine Yvard.

The consultation for both the galleries and the book has been extremely wide. Denny Hemming provided a very constructive and sympathetic editorial service.

The authors are also particularly grateful to the following for their great support throughout: Lothar Bogdanski, Jan Buergel, Susanne Grimm, Cornelia Hoppe, Stefan Kramer, Thomas Schelper (Gipsformerei, Staatliche Museen zu Berlin), Hans Effenberger, Stephanie Exner, Astrid Nielsen (Albertinum, Staatliche Kunstsammlungen Dresden), Kurt van der Basch (film artist), Diane Bilbey (Art UK), Laurence Blyth (independent film-maker), Annarita Caputo (Istituto Statale d'Arte, Florence), Pamela Clark (Royal Archives), Anne Cowne (Lloyd's Register Foundation), Glyn Davies (Museum of London), Patrick Dickinson (independent film-maker), Elizabeth Edwards (University College London/VARI Visiting Professor), David Ellis (Why Not Associates), Franca Falletti (former Director, Galleria dell'Accademia, Florence), Andrea Felice (FeliceCalchi, Rome), Jonathan Fletcher (Plowman Craven), Alistair Grant (V&A/University of Sussex), Al Gury (Pennsylvania Academy of the Fine Arts), Giovanni Hubbard (retired, Istituto Statale d'Arte, Florence), Berthold Just (Stadtschloss/ Humboldtforum), Lorraine Kypiotis (National Art School in Sydney), Mark Jones (former Director, V&A), Kayla Maloyin (Giust Gallery, Woburn, Massachusetts), Giuseppe Rizzo (Uffizi Gallery, Florence), Andy Saunders (AJS Special Process Inspection Ltd), Chris Seagers (Twentieth Century Fox), Irina Skoptsova (Pushkin State Museum of Fine Arts, Moscow), Nele Strobbe (Royal Museums of Art and History, Brussels), Caterina Tiezzi (University of Leicester), Giuliana Videtta (former Director, Accademia di Belle Arti, Florence), Rebecca Wade (Leeds Museums and Galleries/Henry Moore Institute), Paul Williamson (former Keeper of Sculpture, Metalwork, Ceramics and Glass, V&A).

The conservation of the collection has also received huge input from colleges and universities. We very much appreciate the contributions of Batoul Algasra, Jeanne Callanan, India Carpenter, Valentina Gatto, Ona Curto Graupera, Sophie Lerner, Tina Kenward, Christian Kile, Maxwell Malden, Jonida Mecani, Ian Nurock, Catarina da Silva Ramalho (City and Guilds of London Art School), Vanessa Applebaum, Gabrielle Crowther, Rosemary Jeffries, Cyril Maucourant, Miriam Orsini, Emma Payne, Chenya Wang (UCL, Institute of Archaeology), Roberta Boscherini (Istituto Superiore per la Conservazione ed il Restauro, Rome), Camille Devilliers (Institut National du Patrimoine, Paris), Haddon Dine (University of Delaware), Susanna Etyemez (Hochschule für Bildenden Künste Dresden), Laura Goerke (Fachhochschule Hildesheim), Johanna Kaminska (University of Applied Science, Pottsdam), Ingeborg Kroon (Rijksmuseum Conservation Course, Amsterdam), Maggie Ramos (Durham University) and Karma Yeshey (Courtauld Institute of Art).

# Index